Emotional Intelligence Handbook

Practical Techniques for Enhancing Self-Awareness and Managing Stress

Michael T. Bennet

Please consult a licensed professional before attempting any techniques outlined in this book.

By reading this document, the reader agrees that under no circumstances is the author responsible for any losses, direct or indirect, that are incurred as a result of the use of the information contained within this document, including, but not limited to, errors, omissions, or inaccuracies.

Table of Contents

Introduction

The greatest discovery of my generation is that a human being can alter his life by altering his attitudes. –William James

Have you ever felt overwhelmed by your emotions, questioning your decisions and doubting your relationships? You're not alone. In our fast-paced, stress-filled world, feeling lost in a whirlwind of emotions is increasingly common. The pressures of daily life, coupled with the complexities of interpersonal relationships, often leave us feeling drained and defeated. But what if there was a way to manage these feelings effectively so you can understand and control them rather than be controlled by them?

If you found an opportunity to navigate challenges with ease and enhance your personal and professional relationships while achieving your goals without being derailed by stress or anxiety, would you take it? Mastering emotional intelligence gives you that chance to be in control of your life. This book takes you on a path toward understanding the power of your emotions to help you change your life for the better.

As someone who once battled social anxiety, I understand the life-changing power of emotional intelligence firsthand. My journey began at a young age when I became fascinated with human behavior and emotions, and that led me to pursue a degree in psychology, followed by a master's in emotional intelligence. Over the past 20 years, I've dedicated my life to coaching individuals from all walks of life—corporate executives, young adults, people struggling with relationship issues, and those facing intense stress and anxiety.

Throughout my career, I've seen countless individuals who, despite their potential, are held back by their inability to manage emotions effectively. Whether it's a high-stakes meeting at work, a heated argument at home, or an internal battle with self-doubt, the common thread is clear: emotional intelligence is the beginning of true happiness.

This comprehensive guide to developing emotional intelligence focuses on practical techniques and real-life examples. It offers actionable strategies for enhancing self-awareness, managing stress, and improving personal and professional relationships.

Improving your personal and professional relationships requires a deep understanding of empathy and social skills. Empathy promotes healthier relationships by enabling you to communicate effectively and build rapport with others.

You may be seeking personal development or looking for ways to improve your emotional well-being and relationships. Perhaps you're a professional aiming to advance your career by enhancing your leadership skills and team performance. This book provides valuable insights and practical tools to help you achieve your emotional intelligence goals regardless of who you are.

Apart from offering practical techniques, this book also shows the significance of emotional intelligence through relatable real-life examples that demonstrate its impact while providing inspiration and motivation to apply these concepts in your own life. Learning from the experiences of others gives you a deeper understanding of how you can use emotional intelligence to overcome challenges and achieve personal growth.

The journey toward mastering emotional intelligence is a continuous process of self-improvement. This book fosters ongoing personal growth and resilience and equips you with the skills to navigate life's ups and downs effectively.

Join me as we explore the different aspects of emotional intelligence and the skills that will improve your life. Whether you're dealing with stress, facing challenges in your relationships, or striving for professional advancement, I wrote this book with your struggles in mind so that I'd guide you from my experience and years of research.

Your emotional intelligence journey awaits. Dive right in and take the first step toward a more emotionally intelligent and fulfilling life!

Chapter 1: Understanding Emotional Intelligence

It is very important to understand that emotional intelligence is not the opposite of intelligence. It is not the triumph of heart over head; it is the unique intersection of both. –David Caruso

Emotional intelligence (EQ) is an essential aspect of personal and professional development. EQ allows us to confront the complexities of human interactions with greater ease and empathy. Unlike cognitive intelligence (IQ), which focuses on analytical and logical reasoning, EQ encompasses a broader spectrum of skills that delve into self-awareness and social adeptness, making it a vital aspect of our daily lives.

In this chapter, you'll learn about the essential elements of emotional intelligence, including self-awareness, self-regulation, motivation, empathy, and social skills. Each component plays a significant role in fostering both personal growth and professional success. You will learn about practical strategies for recognizing and managing your emotions, as well as how to improve your ability to connect with others. Developing your emotional intelligence equips you to improve communication and build stronger relationships.

What Is Emotional Intelligence?

To begin with, emotional intelligence (EQ) is a term that encapsulates the capacity to perceive, use, understand, manage, and handle emotions effectively (Luna et al., 2021). This foundational skill significantly impacts personal growth and professional success because our emotions play an integral role in how we behave, make decisions, and interact with others. A person with high emotional intelligence can leverage good communication skills and empathy and use them to deal with challenging situations, lead, or motivate others. Individuals with high EQ also excel in personal and work environments by controlling their emotions and understanding others.

Recognizing emotions in oneself and others is an essential component of emotional intelligence. This acknowledgment is necessary for effective communication and social adeptness. When you can accurately identify what you are feeling, it becomes easier to convey those emotions appropriately and constructively. Similarly, recognizing emotions in others enables more empathetic interactions and fosters stronger relationships and better teamwork.

The primary components of emotional intelligence include self-regulation, self-awareness, empathy, social skills, and motivation. Each plays a crucial role in improving personal and professional effectiveness.

Self-Awareness

If you are self-aware, you can monitor your emotional states without being overwhelmed by them. Self-awareness involves being aware of your emotions and how they affect your thoughts and behavior (Drigas et al., 2023). For instance, if you notice that you feel anxious before a big presentation, acknowledging this emotion can help you take steps to manage it, such as practicing deep breathing or rehearsing your speech.

An example of self-awareness in action is when a manager recognizes their frustration during a team meeting. Instead of letting that frustration dictate their response, they acknowledge it internally, choose to pause, and then respond calmly and constructively. This approach maintains a positive work environment while setting a standard for emotional regulation within the team.

Self-Regulation

Closely tied to self-awareness is self-regulation, the ability to manage one's emotions healthily and productively. It entails staying in control when faced with stressful situations and adapting to changing circumstances. Self-regulated individuals do not react impulsively; instead, they think before they act.

For instance, a customer service representative dealing with a difficult customer must exercise self-regulation to remain calm and composed. Managing their immediate impulse to react defensively enables them to provide a thoughtful and helpful response instead of escalating the situation by overreacting. In this example, self-control resolves the issue more efficiently and promotes customer contentment and allegiance.

Motivation

Another critical component of EQ is motivation. This is the drive to achieve external rewards and a deep-seated inner ambition to pursue goals with energy and persistence. People with high emotional intelligence often have a clear sense of purpose and can stay focused on long-term objectives despite setbacks.

For instance, if you are working toward a promotion or better grades, you may face numerous challenges along the way, including increased workload and criticism. However, your intrinsic motivation helps you persevere and learn from obstacles rather than being discouraged by them. This mindset is what propels you toward your goal and inspires those around you to work harder on their targets.

Empathy

Understanding and sharing the emotions of others is another vital aspect of emotional intelligence known as empathy. Empathetic individuals can put themselves in others' shoes, facilitating deeper connections and more meaningful interactions. Understanding and connecting with others goes beyond just feeling sorry for them; it requires actively listening to and appreciating their viewpoints.

The ability to understand and share the feelings of others can manifest in various ways in a work environment. For example, a team leader who senses a team member's unspoken stress might offer support or adjust workloads to alleviate pressure. Such actions build trust and loyalty, making teams more cohesive and collaborative.

Social Skills

Lastly, social skills are a critical aspect of emotional intelligence. These skills encompass a range of abilities, including effective communication, conflict resolution, and relationship management. People with strong social skills can navigate social networks smoothly, build rapport with diverse individuals, and influence others positively.

A practical scenario where social skills are paramount is in negotiation settings. Whether negotiating a contract with a client or mediating a dispute between colleagues, it's important to have the ability to communicate clearly, listen actively, and find mutually beneficial solutions. These skills help you resolve conflicts and pave the way for more productive interactions.

Greater emotional awareness inevitably leads to improved self-management. When you understand your emotions and their triggers, you can develop strategies to manage them better, reducing stress and enhancing overall well-being. For instance, practicing mindfulness can help you stay present and regulate your emotional responses, leading to healthier relationships and increased emotional resilience.

Empathy also plays a pivotal role in strengthening relationships. Understanding and valuing others' emotions helps you create a foundation of trust and respect. This empathetic approach fosters open communication and collaboration, whether in personal friendships or professional partnerships.

What Are the Differences Between IQ and EQ?

In our journey to understand the contrasting natures of IQ and EQ, we must first recognize what each measures and evaluates. As we now know, IQ mainly focuses on cognitive function and analytical abilities. It assesses how well you can use logic and reason, solve mathematical problems, and understand complex ideas. The traditional method for assessing IQ involves evaluating different abilities, including verbal understanding, memory, problem-solving, and cognitive speed. These quantifiable metrics provide a standardized score indicating an individual's intelligence level.

On the other hand, we know that EQ involves emotional understanding and interpersonal skills. Unlike the tangible metrics of IQ, emotional intelligence encompasses awareness of your emotions, the ability to empathize with others, effective communication, conflict resolution, and the capacity to manage relationships judiciously. A renowned psychologist, Daniel Goleman, highlighted five primary components of EQ (Antonopoulou, 2024):

- self-awareness

- social skills
- self-regulation
- empathy
- motivation

As discussed earlier, these components together form a comprehensive view of how emotionally adept an individual is in navigating the complexities of human interactions.

It is becoming increasingly evident in contemporary settings that emotional intelligence holds significant sway over personal success and well-being, often more than traditional IQ scores. For instance, a person with high EQ is better equipped to handle stress because they can recognize their emotional triggers and respond in a balanced manner. This emotional resilience translates to improved mental health, greater job satisfaction, and robust relationships. Conversely, someone may excel intellectually but struggle with managing their emotions, leading to challenges like stress and burnout.

The contrast between high IQ and high EQ becomes palpable when we consider real-life scenarios. Many individuals with high intellectual capabilities might find themselves socially isolated due to difficulties relating to others. High IQ does not automatically equate to social adeptness. You may already know that brilliant minds can sometimes be misunderstood or fail in collaborative environments where teamwork and mutual understanding are paramount. Emotional intelligence bridges this gap by fostering better interpersonal relations. It helps you read social cues, display genuine empathy, and maintain harmonious interactions, all of which are crucial for personal and professional success.

Organizations across various industries have long recognized the importance of hiring individuals with high IQs for roles that require technical prowess and analytical skills. However, there is a noticeable shift toward valuing EQ equally, if not more, during the hiring and promotion processes. Employers find that employees with high emotional intelligence tend to perform better in team settings, exhibit leadership qualities, and contribute positively to workplace culture. An environment where team members understand and support each other's emotional needs tends to be more productive and innovative.

Moreover, cultivating emotional intelligence offers substantial benefits beyond the professional sphere. In personal life, high EQ contributes to healthier, more fulfilling relationships. When you learn to effectively communicate your feelings, show empathy, and navigate conflicts thoughtfully, you are more likely to maintain long-lasting connections with friends, family, and partners. Your EQ lays the foundation for supportive and understanding relationships by helping you build trust and rapport.

In my experience, I have noticed many real-world examples that illustrate the life-changing power of emotional intelligence. This brings me to the story of a top-performing software engineer who struggled with team dynamics. Despite his superior technical skills and impressive IQ, his lack of empathy and poor communication led to frequent misunderstandings and conflicts within the team. After actively working on this problem, he embarked on improving his EQ through workshops and mindfulness practices. His change was remarkable, and the results improved his interactions beyond what he ever thought possible. He became a better listener and could navigate office politics with more ease. His relationships with colleagues improved significantly. As a result, his overall performance and job satisfaction increased, showing how EQ can complement and enhance IQ.

It is also noteworthy that people-focused professions place a high premium on emotional intelligence. Fields such as nursing, teaching, counseling, and social work require practitioners to engage with others empathetically and compassionately constantly. In these vocations, EQ is often the cornerstone of effectiveness and success. An empathetic teacher can understand and address student concerns more effectively, while a nurse with high emotional intelligence can provide comfort and assurance to patients, leading to better patient outcomes.

Ultimately, focusing solely on IQ without cultivating EQ might lead to an imbalanced approach to personal and professional development. While cognitive abilities are essential, especially in fields requiring analytical thinking and problem-solving, emotional intelligence rounds out the skill set needed to thrive in today's interconnected world. Leading a fulfilling life involves more than just intellectual achievements; it requires the ability to connect deeply with others, understand their perspectives, and manage one’s own emotional landscape effectively.

The Impact of EQ on Personal and Professional Success

Emotional intelligence plays a critical role in success across various life domains. One of the most evident ways high EQ individuals stand out is through enhanced communication skills. These individuals are adept at understanding and managing their own emotions as well as perceiving and influencing the feelings of others. This ability makes them exceptional communicators and conflict resolvers, fostering better personal and professional relationships.

Consider how effective communication can transform relationships. High-EQ individuals exhibit empathy, which allows them to connect with others on a deeper level. They listen actively and respond thoughtfully, which reduces misunderstandings and builds trust. For instance, imagine a workplace scenario where two colleagues disagree. A person with high emotional intelligence would approach the situation with calm and clarity, seeking to understand the other person's perspective and addressing the issue without escalating the conflict. This approach resolves the immediate problem and strengthens the overall relationship.

Furthermore, high-EQ individuals are often seen as natural leaders (Cavaness et al., 2020 & Lee et al., 2023). Leadership requires more than technical skills; it demands an understanding of people, motivation, and collaboration. Those with high emotional intelligence excel in these areas. They can navigate complex social dynamics, inspire and motivate their teams, and create an environment where everyone feels valued and heard. This leads to higher morale and improved collaboration within the team. When employees feel understood and appreciated, they are more likely to contribute their best effort and work together harmoniously toward common goals.

Here is a story about Sarah, a manager at a tech company. Early in her career, she faced significant professional setbacks due to her inability to handle stress and conflicts. However, after attending an EQ development workshop, she began implementing the skills she learned. She became more self-aware and learned better ways to manage her stress, and she also started practicing empathetic listening. Over time, these changes improved her personal relationships and even made her an effective leader. Her team's productivity increased, and she was eventually promoted to a senior management position.

Another illustrative example is John, who struggled with maintaining healthy personal relationships. His low awareness of his emotions led to frequent arguments and misunderstandings with his family and friends. After learning about emotional intelligence, he started practicing self-regulation and empathy. He made a conscious effort to understand his loved ones' feelings and respond compassionately. This shift drastically improved his relationships, leading to a happier and more fulfilling personal life.

Another recent article also supports that high EQ is associated with better stress management and overall mental health (Stoewen, 2024). Individuals with high emotional intelligence are more resilient and capable of navigating life's challenges effectively. This resilience translates into better coping strategies, reduced anxiety, and improved overall well-being. As such, the benefits of high EQ extend beyond professional success to encompass a healthier and more balanced life.

Neurological Basis and Science Behind EQ

Understanding the intricate workings of EQ involves delving into the scientific principles rooted in human biology. Emotions are processed in our brains, primarily within an almond-shaped structure known as the amygdala. The amygdala plays a critical role in detecting and responding to emotional stimuli, whether it be fear from a perceived threat or joy from a positive experience.

When you encounter an emotionally charged situation, your amygdala springs into action, often faster than your conscious mind can process. This rapid response is what triggers immediate reactions, such as the fight-or-flight response in stressful situations. Remember, emotional intelligence is about managing your emotions effectively, and this is where the prefrontal cortex comes into play. Located at the front of the brain, the prefrontal cortex assists in regulating these emotional responses, enabling us to evaluate and respond thoughtfully rather than impulsively.

For instance, if someone criticizes you in social settings, your amygdala might trigger a defensive or angry reaction. But with a well-developed prefrontal cortex, you can take a moment to consider the criticism constructively and respond more calmly and rationally. This balance between the amygdala's emotional processing and the prefrontal cortex's regulation is fundamental to emotional intelligence.

One fascinating aspect of our brains that supports the idea of developing EQ skills over time is *b*rain plasticity. The term refers to the brain's capacity to adapt in response to new experiences and environments. This means that while some individuals might naturally have higher levels of EQ, others can cultivate these skills through practice and intentional effort.

If a young professional was just getting started in the workforce, they might struggle with managing stress or resolving conflicts. However, engaging in reflective practices and seeking feedback while exposing themselves to diverse social interactions can gradually enhance their emotional intelligence. Over time, their brain adapts to these experiences, strengthening neural connections that support better emotional regulation and empathy.

High EQ individuals often exhibit remarkable resilience and mental health. This resilience stems from their enhanced capability to manage stress responses effectively. Awareness and regulation are two key components here. When faced with adversity, individuals with high EQ can recognize their emotional state, understand the underlying causes, and employ strategies to manage it. Whether through mindfulness, deep breathing exercises, or simply taking a break, these individuals can navigate stress without becoming overwhelmed.

For example, imagine a healthcare worker on a particularly hectic day. Their patients are numerous, and the demands are relentless. A person with high EQ might take short, mindful pauses between tasks to breathe deeply and reset their focus. They acknowledge the stress but don't allow it to dictate their actions, and this helps them maintain a calm and composed demeanor that benefits both themselves and those around them.

The connection between emotional intelligence and overall psychological health is also well-documented. Studies have shown that individuals with higher EQ tend to have better mental health outcomes (Farrahi et al., 2015 & Moeller et al., 2020). They are generally more satisfied with their lives, experience lower levels of anxiety and depression, and possess stronger coping mechanisms for dealing with life's challenges.

Guidelines for developing EQ could include practicing self-awareness by regularly reflecting on one's emotions and identifying triggers. Another effective method is cultivating empathy by actively listening to others and putting oneself in their shoes. These practices improve personal well-being and also enhance interpersonal relationships and workplace dynamics.

To sum up, the journey to understanding emotional intelligence is an exploration of the interconnectedness of our brain's structures and functions. The amygdala and prefrontal cortex collaborate to manage our emotional experiences and responses. Brain plasticity underscores the potential for continuous growth in EQ skills through meaningful experiences and deliberate practice. High EQ individuals exemplify resilience by effectively managing stress and promoting mental health. Research consistently demonstrates EQ's significant impact on both psychological health and real-world outcomes.

Now that we have explored the essential components of emotional intelligence, it's clear how these skills significantly impact our daily lives. Recognizing, understanding, and managing our emotions enable us to navigate personal and professional challenges more effectively. Cultivating self-awareness, self-regulation, motivation, empathy, and social skills improves our ability to connect with and create a supportive environment at home and in external situations.

Working to improve emotional intelligence is an ongoing process you can achieve over time by implementing strategies like practicing mindfulness, seeking feedback, and actively listening when communicating. Embracing these practices contributes to personal growth and also nurtures a more empathetic and collaborative community around you. Investing in your emotional intelligence paves the way for a more fulfilling life filled with meaningful connections and characterized by resilient handling of life's inevitable ups and downs.

Chapter 2: Enhancing Self-Awareness

The first step toward change is awareness. The second step is acceptance. - Nathaniel Branden

Enhancing self-awareness is a journey that invites us to look inward so we can have a deeper understanding of our emotions and their impacts on our lives. It encourages reflection and introspection, which provides tools designed to help manage our emotional landscapes more effectively. This chapter gives you a gentle nudge toward cultivating this essential skill through age-old practices and modern techniques.

This chapter explores several methods that aid in enhancing self-awareness. First, we will discuss how journaling can unravel complex emotions and serve as a timeline of emotional growth. Next, we explore meditation's power in promoting mental clarity and emotional regulation through mindfulness. The chapter also covers strategies for identifying and managing emotional triggers to equip you to navigate challenging emotions. It also suggests daily self-check-ins and vocabulary exercises to consistently maintain and deepen your emotional insight. Through these techniques, you will be better equipped to work toward a deeper connection with yourself as you brace to face life's vicissitudes with resilience.

The Benefits of Journaling for Self-Awareness

Journaling can be a powerful tool for enhancing self-awareness. It allows you to process your emotions thoroughly by providing a dedicated space for reflection. One of the most significant benefits of journaling is its ability to distill complex emotions into clearer thoughts. When you write about your feelings, you engage in a form of cognitive processing that can transform overwhelming emotions into more manageable and understandable constructs. This clarity often leads to better emotional understanding, which prepares you to handle your feelings more effectively.

Moreover, keeping a journal is a valuable record of personal growth and emotional changes over time. As you look back on past entries, patterns emerge, giving insights into how you have evolved emotionally. This retrospective view can show how certain situations previously triggered intense emotions but no longer have the same impact. Observing these changes can be empowering and encouraging, reinforcing a sense of progress and resilience.

In addition to fostering emotional clarity and tracking personal growth, journaling can relieve stress. The simple act of writing about what bothers us can help alleviate the intensity of those emotions. It's a way of venting—externalizing internal turmoil onto the page, which can then make problems seem less daunting. This process not only reduces stress but aids in calming our minds, creating a sense of relief and release. Articulating your worries and fears helps reduce their power over you.

Another significant advantage of journaling is its capacity to support emotional accountability and personal growth by outlining future aspirations. When you commit your goals and dreams to paper, you create a tangible plan and a psychological commitment. This act encourages you to reflect on your current state versus where you want to be, which then prompts introspection and self-assessment. It helps keep you focused on your objectives and enables you to track progress while staying motivated. Not only does this bolster your sense of purpose, but it also enhances your ambition and drive.

To delve deeper, let's consider how journaling brings about emotional clarity. When faced with a jumble of conflicting feelings, putting pen to paper forces you to slow down and figure out exactly what you are experiencing. For instance, rather than remaining mired in anger or frustration after an argument, writing about the incident can help disentangle the various emotions involved—perhaps sadness, disappointment, or even fear. When you break down these emotions, you can understand their roots and address them individually, which leads to more effective emotional regulation.

Journaling's role as a diary of emotional growth can't be underestimated. Over time, consistent journaling provides a comprehensive narrative of our emotional landscape. This written record becomes a mirror reflecting our inner world, showing us how different experiences shape our emotional responses. For example, revisiting journal entries from a year ago can reveal how challenges that once seemed insurmountable were overcome, demonstrating our capacity for resilience and adaptability. Such reflections can offer valuable lessons and reminders of our strength, helping us navigate current emotional challenges with greater confidence.

As a stress-relief tool, journaling offers immediate and long-term benefits. In the short term, writing down stressful events or feelings can be cathartic, reducing their immediate impact. When you experience stress, your natural reaction may be to ruminate or let emotions simmer internally, which can exacerbate the situation. However, if you channel those feelings into words, you create a structured outlet that can provide relief and a moment of calm. Over the long term, regular journaling practices can build emotional resilience and help you better manage stress when it arises.

Outlining future aspirations in a journal is a proactive step toward achieving personal growth. When you write about your hopes and ambitions, you engage in a form of self-prompting that keeps your goals at the forefront of your mind. This practice encourages frequent reflection on your actions and decisions, ensuring they align with your larger objectives. For example, if you aspire to improve your work-life balance, regularly journaling about related efforts and experiences can help you maintain focus and adjust strategies as needed to achieve that goal.

Making journaling a habit presents continuous benefits because each entry becomes an opportunity to pause and reflect. It offers moments of self-awareness that you might otherwise overlook in the busyness of daily life. This ongoing practice nurtures a deeper connection with your emotions and fosters an environment where self-discovery and growth can flourish. The cumulative effect of these small, regular reflections can lead to significant shifts in how you perceive and manage your emotional well-being.

The Role of Meditation in Self-Awareness

Meditation offers a powerful method to enhance self-awareness, primarily by promoting mental clarity and emotional regulation. One fundamental benefit of meditation is its ability to reduce mental clutter. If you tend to have hectic days, your mind may become overwhelmed with an unending stream of thoughts and concerns. These distractions can impede your ability to reflect effectively on your emotions and actions. Through regular meditation practice, you can learn to quiet the mind and create a space where focus and clarity can flourish. This enhanced focus allows for deeper self-reflection by helping you gain a clearer understanding of your internal experiences.

In addition to reducing mental clutter, meditation fosters a meaningful connection between emotions and physical sensations. During meditation, you often engage in body scans or mindful breathing exercises, which encourage you to notice how different emotions manifest physically. For example, anxiety might present as a tightness in the chest, while happiness could feel like a lightness in the shoulders. Recognizing these physical cues helps you become more attuned to your emotional states and responses. This heightened awareness facilitates healthier emotional responses, enabling you to address your feelings before they escalate into more significant issues.

Moreover, practicing mindfulness—a key component of many meditation techniques—allows you to observe your thoughts without judgment. Mindfulness teaches that thoughts are transient and do not define one's identity. Adopting a non-judgmental perspective helps you view your thoughts as temporary events rather than fixed realities. This shift in perception reduces impulsivity because you learn to pause and reflect before reacting to your thoughts or emotions. It creates a buffer between stimulus and response, enabling more deliberate and thoughtful decision-making.

Another critical aspect of meditation is its role in managing difficult emotions by decreasing emotional reactivity. Emotional reactivity occurs when you respond intensely and immediately to emotional triggers, often leading to regrettable actions or words. Through meditation, you can develop a sense of equanimity—a balanced, calm state of mind that enables you to navigate challenging emotions with greater ease. Regular meditation practice helps build resilience, which allows you to experience and process emotions without becoming overwhelmed.

Reflecting on past entries can assist in evaluating growth and setbacks, providing valuable insights into one's emotional journey. For instance, you might notice patterns in your reactions to certain situations, which helps you identify areas for improvement. Recognizing these patterns through meditation can guide personal development efforts, making it an invaluable tool for enhancing self-awareness.

Using prompts during meditation sessions can guide you toward deeper self-awareness. Prompts may include questions like "What am I feeling right now?" or "What thoughts keep recurring?" Such inquiries encourage introspection and help you delve into the root causes of your emotions. This process boosts self-awareness and empowers you to address underlying issues constructively.

Emily, a marketing executive dealing with high stress at work, had trouble adjusting because her days were filled with constant tension and a relentless pace, which left her emotionally exhausted. Upon incorporating meditation into her routine, she began to notice significant changes. Sarah learned to declutter her mind by dedicating just 20 minutes each morning to meditation, which fostered a sense of calm throughout her day. She became more attuned to her body's signals and recognized that the tightness in her shoulder was a manifestation of her anxiety. Acknowledging this link allowed her to take proactive steps, such as deep breathing exercises, whenever she sensed the onset of stress.

Another woman, let's call her Sheryl, used mindfulness to help curtail her impulsive reactions during stressful meetings. Instead of snapping at colleagues, she paused, took a moment to observe her thoughts, and responded thoughtfully. This shift in behavior improved her workplace relationships and bolstered her leadership skills. Her ability to manage her emotions effectively set a positive example for her team, which fostered a more harmonious work environment.

Regular meditation also transformed Sheryl's approach to challenging emotions. She no longer felt engulfed by these feelings when faced with intense frustration or disappointment. Instead, she approached them with curiosity, exploring their origins and learning from them. This newfound resilience made her more adept at dealing with professional setbacks and personal conflicts, ultimately enhancing her overall well-being.

Sheryl's journey highlights the immense power of meditation in enhancing self-awareness. Integrating mindfulness techniques into daily routines gives you similar benefits, including mental clarity, emotional regulation, and a deeper understanding of yourself. Meditation is a practical and accessible tool for anyone seeking to improve their emotional intelligence and lead a more balanced life.

You don't need extensive resources or prior experience to start a meditation practice. Simple guided meditations, readily available through various apps and online platforms, offer an excellent entry point. Setting aside even a few minutes each day can make a substantial difference over time. As you become more comfortable with the practice, you can experiment with techniques such as loving-kindness meditation or visualization to further enhance your self-awareness.

Identifying and Managing Emotional Triggers

Understanding and managing emotional triggers is a cornerstone of self-awareness. Emotional triggers are specific experiences or stimuli that evoke strong emotional reactions, often linked to past experiences or unresolved issues. These triggers play a significant role in your emotional responses, and understanding them is crucial for proactive emotional management.

Identifying your triggers begins with recognizing the situations, people, or environments that cause intense emotional reactions. For example, you might notice that criticism at work provokes feelings of anger or frustration. Pinpointing these triggers enables you to anticipate your reactions and prepare strategies to manage them effectively. Recognizing these patterns allows you to take control of your emotions rather than letting them control you. Understanding the significance of emotional triggers also helps create a foundation for better emotional regulation.

One powerful tool for tracking and understanding emotional reactions is journaling. Writing down your thoughts and feelings provides an outlet for expressing emotions and identifying patterns. When you journal regularly, you start noticing recurring themes and situations that trigger certain emotional responses. This practice clarifies underlying issues and enables you to anticipate and prepare for similar situations. For instance, if you observe that social gatherings often lead to anxiety, you can develop coping mechanisms such as deep-breathing exercises or positive self-talk to manage those feelings more effectively.

Journaling also serves as a reflective practice that offers insights into how your emotions evolve over time. When you revisit past entries, you better understand your emotional journey and progress. This continuous reflection fosters deeper self-awareness and emotional intelligence, allowing you to respond more thoughtfully in challenging situations. The act of writing itself can be therapeutic as it provides a safe space to explore and process complex emotions.

Role-playing exercises are another valuable technique for managing emotional triggers. With role-playing, you can practice and refine your reactions in a controlled environment by simulating potential scenarios that might provoke an emotional response. This approach prepares you for real-life situations, enhancing your confidence and ability to handle them maturely. For instance, if public speaking triggers anxiety, rehearsing your speech in front of a mirror or with a supportive friend can help you manage those feelings and improve your performance.

Mindfulness techniques are essential for managing emotional triggers when they arise. Mindfulness involves staying present and fully engaging with the current moment without judgment. Practicing mindfulness creates a buffer between stimulus and response by cultivating awareness of your thoughts and emotions. This space allows you to choose how to react rather than reacting impulsively.

One effective mindfulness technique is deep breathing exercises. When faced with an emotional trigger, taking slow, deep breaths helps activate the body's relaxation response, reducing stress and calming the mind. Another technique is body scanning, where you focus on different parts of your body, releasing tension and grounding yourself in the present moment. These practices help maintain a calm perspective, allowing you to respond to triggers with greater clarity and composure.

Additionally, incorporating mindfulness into your daily routine can enhance your overall emotional resilience. Regular meditation or mindful activities, such as yoga or walking in nature, reinforce your ability to stay grounded and centered. These practices build a reservoir of inner calm you can draw upon during challenging times, promoting better emotional regulation and self-awareness.

Daily Self-Check-Ins and Emotional Vocabulary Exercises

You can start by establishing a routine for daily emotional assessments to improve your self-awareness. When you take time each day to check in and assess your emotional state, you begin to hold yourself accountable for your emotions. This can be as simple as setting aside a few minutes in the morning or evening to reflect on how you feel and why these feelings may have arisen. Consistency is key, so you'll want to make this a regular practice to promote a deeper understanding of your emotional landscape over time.

Developing an emotional vocabulary is another essential step in enhancing self-awareness. We often settle for basic descriptors like "happy," "sad," or "angry," which don't fully capture the complexity of our emotional experiences. However, when you expand your emotional vocabulary, it becomes easier to recognize exactly what you are feeling. Words like "frustrated," "hopeful," or "overwhelmed" provide more accurate representations of emotional states. The ability to name emotions precisely helps in recognizing patterns in your emotional responses and fosters better communication with others about one's internal experiences.

One excellent tool for developing an emotional vocabulary and exploring complex emotions is the emotion wheel. The emotion wheel categorizes emotions into primary feelings such as joy, sadness, anger, and fear and further breaks these down into more nuanced emotions. For instance, "joy" can encompass emotions like "optimism," "pride," or "contentment." Using this wheel regularly can help individuals pinpoint their exact feelings more accurately than they might with words alone. It acts as a guide to dissecting and understanding one's emotions on a deeper level, enabling clearer communication and more effective emotional management.

Reflective practices play a crucial role in enhancing emotional awareness. These practices could involve meditation, mindful breathing exercises, or simply sitting quietly and reflecting on your day. Through reflection, you can identify specific emotional experiences, understand your triggers, and recognize how these emotions impact your thoughts and behaviors. Reflective practices create a space for introspection by allowing you to process your emotions constructively rather than reactively. This proactive approach to emotional management leads to greater emotional stability and resilience over time.

Emotionally aware individuals are often better equipped to handle stress, navigate interpersonal relationships, and lead effectively in professional settings. Establishing a routine for daily emotional assessments helps lay the groundwork for this awareness. Consider beginning your day with a mental scan: How do you feel physically and emotionally? Are there specific events or thoughts contributing to your current emotional state? Acknowledge these emotions without judgment. Simply observe them. This practice cultivates mindfulness, a critical component of emotional intelligence.

Expanding your vocabulary to include a rich array of emotional terms does more than just aid personal insight. It also improves interactions with others. When you can express your feelings clearly, it lessens misunderstandings and makes conflict resolution more straightforward. Imagine explaining to a colleague that you're feeling "anxious about the upcoming presentation" rather than saying you're "stressed." The former conveys precise information and opens up possibilities for support and empathy.

The emotion wheel serves as a visual aid that guides you through the labyrinth of your emotions. Next time you're unsure of what you're feeling, consider taking a moment to consult the wheel. You might find that what you thought was anger is actually frustration combined with disappointment. This nuanced understanding provides clarity and helps in forming a strategic approach to managing those emotions. Maybe you realize that a conversation with a friend or a short walk might alleviate some of that compounded tension.

Incorporating reflective practices may sound a little complicated in the beginning, but something as simple as keeping a journal where you jot down a few lines about your day can suffice. What emotions stood out today? Were there specific triggers? How did you handle them? Writing these reflections helps identify recurring patterns and themes in your emotional life. Over time, these observations can reveal valuable insights about your emotional triggers and how best to manage them.

When seeking personal development, you may find that these practices contribute immensely to improving your emotional intelligence. Better emotional awareness can reduce stress, enhance relationships, and increase overall well-being. If you are a professional looking to advance your career, you should note that emotional intelligence is highly valued in the workplace. Leaders who understand their own emotions and those of their team members stand a better chance of encouraging a more harmonious and productive work environment. If you are grappling with relationship challenges or anxiety, these strategies offer practical tools for managing emotions more effectively, which leads to healthier interactions and improved mental health.

A rich emotional vocabulary also benefits younger individuals who are learning to deal with emotions. Teaching children to express their feelings accurately and without shame sets them up for a lifetime of emotional health and resilience. Encouraging them to describe their feelings in detail helps normalize emotional expression and reduces the stigma surrounding certain emotions. You can also gradually introduce reflective practices. Start small—perhaps with a five-minute reflection at the end of the day—and slowly build from there. The goal is to make these practices sustainable and enjoyable so they become a natural part of your daily routine rather than a chore.

In this chapter, we explored various techniques you can use to boost self-awareness, specifically through journaling and meditation. Journaling provides a constructive outlet for expressing emotions by breaking down complex feelings into clear thoughts. Documenting your emotional journey gives you valuable insights into your growth and resilience over time. Meditation complements this by offering mental clarity and emotional regulation. Through mindfulness practices, you can observe your thoughts and reactions without judgment, and that creates room for healthier responses to emotional triggers.

Journaling and meditation consistently create a solid foundation for emotional self-awareness. These tools enable you to process emotions, manage stress, and set realistic goals for personal development. They offer practical ways to improve your well-being and navigate life's complexities with greater ease, whether you're an adult seeking to improve your emotional intelligence, a professional aiming to advance your career, or someone facing challenges with anxiety or relationships.

Chapter 3: Managing Stress Effectively

It's not the load that breaks you down; it's the way you carry it. –Lou Holtz

Effective stress management is essential for maintaining both mental and physical well-being. In our fast-paced world, stress has become a prevalent part of daily life, affecting our health, relationships, and productivity. As you work to develop effective strategies for managing stress, it's imperative that you understand its intricacies as well as how it influences your body and mind. You can dive deep into the physiological mechanisms behind stress and explore its early symptoms to arm yourself with the knowledge needed to counteract its negative impact.

This chapter explores various aspects of stress management, starting with an in-depth look at the body's natural response to stress. We will examine the fight-or-flight mechanism and its implications on our daily lives, highlighting how chronic stress can lead to severe health issues. The chapter also explores practical techniques such as mindfulness practices and physical activities that can help alleviate stress. Understanding individual differences in stress perception and building resilience equips you with comprehensive strategies to handle stress more efficiently. This holistic approach promotes a balanced lifestyle and improves your emotional intelligence.

Understanding the Physiology of Stress

The human body's response to stress is a deeply ingrained physiological reaction that has evolved over millennia. Understanding this response is crucial for anyone looking to manage stress effectively. As mentioned earlier, when you encounter a stressful situation, your body initiates what is known as the fight-or-flight response. This neurobiological mechanism involves activating the sympathetic-adreno-medullary (SAM) axis and the hypothalamic-pituitary-adrenal (HPA) axis. These systems work in tandem to prepare your body to either confront or flee from perceived danger.

During the fight-or-flight response, the adrenal glands release adrenaline and cortisol into the bloodstream, causing increased heart rate and elevated blood pressure. Simultaneously, non-essential functions, such as digestion, slow down to allow the body to focus on the immediate threat. This interplay between various systems is designed to facilitate physical performance in critical situations, but it can become problematic when activated too often or for prolonged periods.

Recognizing the physical symptoms of stress early on is vital for timely intervention. Common indicators include increased heart rate, sweaty palms, muscle tension, and shallow breathing. These symptoms serve as warning signs that the body is under stress. Being attuned to these signals enables you to take proactive steps to mitigate the effects before they escalate. Techniques such as deep breathing exercises or a short walk can help activate the parasympathetic nervous system, which promotes relaxation and counteracts the stress response.

When stress becomes chronic, it can lead to significant long-term consequences. Prolonged exposure to stress hormones like cortisol can result in physical and emotional exhaustion.

Constantly elevated cortisol levels suppress the immune system, making the body more susceptible to illnesses. Chronic stress also contributes to cardiovascular problems, including high blood pressure and an increased risk of heart attacks. Mental health also suffers because chronic stress often contributes to conditions such as anxiety and depression.

Everyone experiences stress differently, and individual differences in stress perception play a crucial role in how people respond. Some might view a challenging situation as a manageable task, while others may see it as overwhelming. These perceptions can be influenced by various factors, including past experiences, personality traits, and even genetic predispositions. For instance, two individuals facing the same workload might have entirely different stress responses based on their coping mechanisms and resilience.

Past experiences significantly shape how individuals perceive and react to stress. Someone who has faced and overcome previous challenges successfully is likely to view new stressors as less threatening. On the other hand, those who have had negative experiences may find similar situations more daunting. Personality traits also influence stress perception. Traits like optimism and a positive outlook can buffer against stress, making individuals more resilient. Conversely, those prone to negativity or anxiety might find stress harder to manage.

Genetic factors also play a role in stress perception. Specific genes can affect how the brain processes stress signals, which influences an individual's overall stress response. Research indicates that gene variations related to serotonin regulation, for example, can make some people more vulnerable to stress (Weger & Sandi, 2018). Understanding these individual differences is crucial for developing personalized stress management strategies.

Given the complex nature of the stress response, it's clear that managing stress effectively requires a multifaceted approach. One crucial aspect is recognizing and addressing the physiological symptoms early on. Another is understanding the long-term effects of chronic stress and taking steps to prevent it. Lastly, acknowledging individual differences in stress perception allows for tailored strategies that cater to specific needs.

Mindfulness for Stress Reduction

Stress has become a constant companion for many in today's busy and ever-changing world. Mindfulness emerges as a powerful practice to manage this stress and promote mental clarity. It offers scientifically backed techniques that help individuals confront the complexities of modern life.

Mindfulness refers to the practice of being fully present in the moment, aware of where you are and what you are doing, without being overly reactive or overwhelmed by the surrounding environment. We can trace its roots back to ancient Buddhist meditation practices, but today, mindfulness is widely embraced in various secular contexts, including healthcare, education, and personal development. The essence of mindfulness lies in observing your thoughts and emotions without judgment, which then gives you a sense of calm and clarity amidst chaos.

Historically, mindfulness was primarily practiced within spiritual traditions in the East. However, Western scientists and psychologists have extensively studied it over the past few decades to discover more. Researchers have found its significant impact on reducing stress and boosting overall well-being. For instance, renowned mindfulness programs like Mindfulness-Based Stress Reduction (MBSR), developed by Jon Kabat-Zinn in the late 1970s, have shown significant benefits in managing stress, anxiety, and depression (Kriakous et al., 2020).

Research has shown that regular mindfulness practice can lower cortisol levels, the body's primary stress hormone (Turakitwanakan et al., 2013). In addition, mindfulness has been found to increase gray matter density in brain regions associated with learning, memory, and emotional regulation. Studies also indicate that mindfulness can improve psychological processes.

According to Parsons et al. (2021), mindfulness-based interventions have demonstrated success in treating depression, anxiety, and stress among students in health-related fields. These findings underscore the potential of mindfulness to enhance cognitive and behavioral functions, making it a valuable tool for stress management.

Moreover, a study by Worthen & Cash (2023) highlights how mindfulness can lead to better emotional processing. It enables individuals to respond rather than react to stressors, fostering a calmer and more measured approach to life's challenges. This shift from a reactive to a responsive mindset is crucial for maintaining emotional balance.

Mindfulness Techniques

You can employ some practical techniques to effectively incorporate mindfulness into your life without disrupting your daily routines.

Focused breathing is one of the simplest yet most effective mindfulness techniques. It involves paying close attention to your breath, noticing the inhalation and exhalation, and gently bringing your mind back whenever it wanders. Practicing focused breathing for just a few minutes each day can significantly reduce stress levels and promote relaxation.

Meditation is another core technique. It involves setting aside dedicated time to sit quietly and focus on the present moment. A common type of mindfulness meditation is "guided meditation," where an instructor leads you through the practice. Regular meditation enhances self-awareness, reduces negative emotions, and improves emotional resilience.

Body scan meditation is another helpful method for practicing mindfulness. It involves focusing on different parts of your body, usually starting from your toes and moving up to your head. This practice helps release tension and contributes to a deeper connection between the mind and body by paying attention to physical sensations without judgment.

When starting mindfulness, you may want to start small. For example, you can begin with just a few minutes of mindful breathing each day, then slowly increase the duration as you become more comfortable. Create a distraction-free environment for your meditation practice, and aim to practice mindfulness at the same time each day to build a routine.

It's also important to be patient with yourself. It's natural for the mind to wander, so when it does, reach inward and gently bring your focus back without self-criticism.

Incorporating Mindfulness Into Daily Life

Integrating mindfulness into everyday activities doesn't require significant lifestyle changes. Simple strategies such as mindful eating make a huge difference. You can start by paying attention to the sensory experience of eating. Take in the taste, texture, and aroma of your food. Eating mindfully increases the enjoyment of food, promotes better digestion, and reduces overeating.

Mindfulness can be as simple as focusing on the sensation of your feet touching the ground as you walk; the rhythm of your steps and the feeling of the air against your skin become a meditative experience.

When engaging in conversations, you can practice active listening by giving your full attention to the speaker without planning your response while they're talking. This improves communication and strengthens relationships because the other people feel heard, and it allows you time to respond mindfully without hurting others.

You can start by incorporating mindfulness into daily activities, such as eating or walking, and then use alarms or notes to remind yourself to practice mindfulness throughout the day. At the end of each day, take a few moments to reflect on how mindfulness has impacted your stress levels and emotional clarity. As you become more comfortable, you can integrate mindfulness into more aspects of your daily routine.

Physical Activities to Relieve Stress

Physical activity is a cornerstone of effective stress management, offering numerous benefits for mental and physical health. The connection between the body and mind is significant when it comes to handling stress, and engaging in regular exercise plays a pivotal role in promoting overall well-being.

Understanding the mind-body connection is crucial in recognizing how physical activity impacts mental health. Exercise stimulates the production of *endorphins*, often referred to as "feel-good" neurotransmitters, which help elevate mood and reduce feelings of anxiety. This process aids in combating the adverse effects of stress by promoting a sense of relaxation and positivity. Regular physical activity also encourages better sleep patterns, essential for mitigating stress and ensuring the body has adequate rest to recover from daily pressures.

Exercise also acts as a form of active meditation. Activities such as running, swimming, or cycling require focus on movement and breathing, allowing individuals to disconnect from daily worries and immerse themselves in the present moment. This concentration promotes a clearer and calmer mindset by alleviating mental clutter.

I understand it can be difficult to pick which activities to incorporate into your routine, but there are a variety of exercises that contribute to stress management. Aerobic exercises such as running, cycling, and swimming increase heart rate and improve cardiovascular health while boosting endorphin levels. Strength training, including weightlifting and resistance exercises, enhances physical strength and provides a structured routine to instill a sense of accomplishment and control.

Yoga and Pilates are particularly beneficial for stress reduction because they emphasize controlled breathing, mindfulness, and flexibility. These practices integrate physical movement with meditative techniques, helping to balance the mind and body. Yoga, in particular, promotes relaxation through poses and stretches that release muscle tension and improve circulation.

Creating a Routine

Incorporating physical activity into a busy schedule may seem daunting, but several strategies can make it more manageable. One effective approach is to start small. Short bursts of exercise, even 10-minute walks during breaks, can accumulate significant benefits throughout the day. Interval training, which involves alternating between high-intensity activity and rest periods, is another efficient method that maximizes workout benefits in shorter timeframes.

Another strategy is to find activities that you genuinely enjoy. You can take your pick from dancing, hiking, or playing a sport you love. Choosing fun exercises increases the likelihood of making them a regular part of your routine. You can also consider socializing your workouts to add a layer of commitment and more fun. One simple example is planning to meet friends or family for a walk or a gym session.

Developing a consistent exercise routine requires setting realistic goals and steadily building intensity. It's important not to view exercise as a chore but as an integral part of self-care. Scheduling specific times for physical activity, just like any other important task, can help make it a non-negotiable part of the day.

As you work on establishing your physical activity routine, you may also consider interacting with others who have similar goals and hearing about their successes for motivation. For instance, Jane, a working mother of two, struggled with anxiety and sleepless nights due to job demands and family responsibilities. However, when she integrated yoga classes into her weekly routine with the help of a friend, she found a significant decrease in her anxiety levels and saw improvements in her sleep quality. The mindfulness and breathing techniques she learned in yoga helped her manage stressful situations more calmly and effectively.

Similarly, Tom, an executive at a high-stress firm, went on short runs during his lunch breaks and reported feeling more energized and less overwhelmed by work tasks. Over time, he noticed that his overall mood improved, and he felt better equipped to handle the pressures of his job.

These success stories go on and on, but they show the potential of physical activity in stress management. You, too, can leverage various forms of exercise and set yourself up for significant improvements in mental and physical health.

Building Resilience and Healthy Coping Mechanisms

Resilience is the capacity to bounce back from challenges and adversity in such a way that you adapt positively despite stress. When it comes to emotional intelligence and stress management, resilience is a crucial skill that enables you to navigate life's ups and downs with a sense of control and optimism. It is not about avoiding difficulties but developing the strength and flexibility to respond effectively when they arise. Emotional resilience incorporates self-awareness, realistic optimism, and the ability to regulate your emotions even in trying situations.

Strategies for Building Resilience

Building resilience involves cultivating habits and mindsets that empower you to cope with stress positively. Here are some effective strategies:

- **Positive self-talk:** How you talk to yourself significantly impacts your overall resilience. Instead of focusing on negative thoughts, practice replacing them with affirming statements. For instance, if faced with a setback, instead of thinking, "I can't handle this," try rephrasing it to, "I will find a way to overcome this challenge."

- **Gratitude**: Developing a habit of gratitude shifts your focus from what's going wrong to appreciating what's going right. Keeping a gratitude journal where you list things you're thankful for can enhance your emotional resilience by fostering a positive outlook on life. According to research, gratitude can improve psychological well-being by reducing toxic emotions and increasing happiness (Chowdhury, 2019).

- **Perspective shifts**: Our perception of a situation can often magnify its stress. Learning to view challenges as temporary and solvable rather than insurmountable can mitigate stress. For example, seeing a job loss not as an opportunity to explore new career paths can transform the experience more positively than if you thought of it as a failure.

Healthy Coping Mechanisms

To manage stress effectively, it's essential to develop healthy coping mechanisms. These include problem-solving, seeking support, and setting boundaries. Let's look at each:

- **Problem-solving:** Facing issues head-on by identifying the problem, brainstorming possible solutions, and taking actionable steps can reduce feelings of helplessness. Creating a plan and breaking down tasks into manageable steps can make daunting challenges feel more achievable.

- **Seeking support:** It is vital to surround yourself with a supportive network of friends, family, or professionals. Sharing your concerns with others can provide different perspectives and emotional relief. It's important to recognize when you need help and not hesitate to reach out for support.

- **Setting boundaries:** Establishing personal boundaries helps prevent burnout and balance work, family, and self-care. Learning to say no when necessary and prioritizing tasks can help manage time and energy more effectively, creating space to recharge and reflect.

Developing a Growth Mindset

A growth mindset, coined by psychologist Carol Dweck, refers to the belief that abilities and intelligence can be developed through dedication and hard work (Suman, 2023). This way of thinking encourages viewing challenges as opportunities for growth rather than insurmountable obstacles.

- **Embracing challenges:** Individuals with a growth mindset see difficult tasks as an opportunity to learn and improve. They understand that effort leads to mastery. When confronted with a challenging project, try to approach it with curiosity and willingness to learn instead of shying away or feeling defeated.

- **Learning from criticism:** Constructive criticism is seen not as a personal attack but as valuable feedback for improvement. Adopting this perspective allows you to grow and adapt based on others' insights.

- **Persistence in the face of setbacks:** Persistence is key to resilience. A growth mindset promotes perseverance by framing setbacks as an essential part of the learning process. Each failure is viewed as a stepping stone towards eventual success.

- **Celebrating effort over outcome:** Recognizing and rewarding the process and effort rather than just the outcome fosters a healthy attitude towards continuous improvement. This approach not only builds resilience but also sustains motivation.

Integrating these strategies into daily life can seem daunting at first, but small, consistent efforts can lead to significant changes over time. For instance, you can start by dedicating a few minutes each day to practice positive self-talk or maintain a daily gratitude journal. Seek out a mentor or coach who can provide guidance and support as you navigate stressful situations. Gradually work on setting and maintaining boundaries by assessing your priorities and commitments regularly.

Moreover, adopting a reflective practice, such as journaling about your experiences and responses to stress, provides deeper insights into your resilience journey. Make time to reflect on past challenges, identify the strengths you drew upon to overcome them, and acknowledge the progress you've made. Engaging in mindfulness practices, such as meditation or deep breathing exercises, can further improve your ability to stay grounded and focused during stressful times.

Understanding stress and learning to manage it is crucial for maintaining overall well-being. Recognizing the physiological symptoms of stress, such as increased heart rate and muscle tension, enables you to take timely action to mitigate its effects. Practicing mindfulness helps you stay present and calm, which reduces the impact of day-to-day stressors. You can incorporate physical activities into your routine to further alleviate stress by releasing endorphins, improving mood, and promoting better sleep patterns. It's essential to find activities you enjoy and to start small, gradually building up consistency in your routine.

Building resilience involves developing habits and mindsets that empower you to cope with stress effectively. Positive self-talk, gratitude, and perspective shifts enable you to view challenges more constructively. Healthy coping mechanisms like problem-solving, seeking support, and setting boundaries help maintain balance and prevent burnout. Adopting a growth mindset encourages you to see challenges as opportunities for learning and improvement. Once you integrate these strategies into your daily life, you become better equipped to handle stress and challenge the challenging times life throws at you.

Chapter 4: Empathy and Social Skills

Empathy is about finding echoes of another person in yourself. –Mohsin Hamid

Empathy and social skills are fundamental to forming meaningful connections and improving interpersonal relationships. Empathy, which is the ability to understand and share the feelings of others, acts as a bridge that connects individuals on a deeper emotional level. Social skills, encompassing behaviors such as active listening, effective communication, and conflict resolution, are equally vital in navigating the complexities of human interactions. Together, these two components play a pivotal role in fostering trust, reducing misunderstandings, and creating a supportive environment where everyone feels valued.

In this chapter, we will explore the different aspects of empathy, including cognitive and emotional empathy, and discuss how they contribute to stronger bonds. We will explore practical strategies to cultivate these skills, such as active listening, perspective-taking, and self-reflection. The chapter will also offer insights into how empathy can enhance personal and professional relationships, create a more harmonious atmosphere, and even serve as a buffer against stress. Through relatable examples and actionable advice, you will gain a comprehensive understanding of how to develop your empathetic abilities and improve your social skills, ultimately leading to healthier, more fulfilling interactions.

Defining and Developing Empathy

Empathy is an important aspect of emotional intelligence, and it plays a crucial role in your interpersonal relationships. It involves both understanding and sharing the feelings of others. This ability to connect on an emotional level helps build stronger bonds and fosters a sense of community and belonging.

There are two primary types of empathy: cognitive empathy and emotional empathy. Cognitive empathy refers to the ability to understand another person's perspective or mental state. It allows you to put yourself in someone else's shoes and see things from their point of view. This type of empathy is essential for effective communication and problem-solving, as it enables you to anticipate how others might feel or react in different situations.

On the other hand, emotional empathy involves actually sharing the emotions of another person. It's the sensation you get when you truly feel what someone else is feeling, whether it's joy, sorrow, anger, or frustration. Emotional empathy creates a deep sense of connection and compassion, and that motivates you to support those in need.

Understanding that empathy is a skill you can nurture is empowering. This means you can take active steps to improve your empathetic abilities and, consequently, your overall emotional intelligence. Engaging in specific exercises and activities can significantly improve your capacity for empathy.

One effective method to cultivate empathy is through active listening. Active listening goes beyond merely hearing words; it involves fully concentrating, understanding, responding, and remembering what is being said. When you listen actively, you give the speaker our full attention, showing them that you value their thoughts and feelings. This practice helps you better understand the speaker's emotions and perspectives, and it also demonstrates your respect and willingness to engage meaningfully.

Another technique to develop empathy is perspective-taking. This involves imagining oneself in another person's situation, considering their thoughts, feelings, and experiences. Perspective-taking broadens your understanding of different viewpoints and promotes your ability to connect with others on a deeper level. It encourages you to move beyond your own biases and judgments, which creates room for greater openness and acceptance.

Self-reflection is also a powerful tool for enhancing empathy. Taking the time to reflect on your own emotional responses can provide valuable insights into your behavior and reactions. Examining how you feel in various situations and questioning why you respond in certain ways helps you develop a greater awareness of your own emotions and how they influence your interactions with others. This self-awareness is a critical component of emotional intelligence and helps you become more attuned to the feelings of those around you.

The benefits of cultivating empathy extend far beyond personal growth. Empathy improves personal and professional relationships by creating stronger social connections and reducing misunderstandings. When you approach interactions with empathy, you are more likely to resolve conflicts amicably and build trust with others. In the workplace, empathetic leaders and colleagues contribute to a positive and collaborative environment where individuals feel supported and valued.

Moreover, empathy serves as a buffer against stress. When you are empathetic, you can understand and address the needs of others more effectively, which reduces tension and favors a peaceful environment. Empathy enables you to provide emotional support to those who are struggling so that you can help alleviate their distress and create a more supportive and caring atmosphere.

In personal relationships, empathy deepens your connections with loved ones. Truly understanding and sharing their emotions offers genuine support and comfort and strengthens your bond. Empathy promotes healthy and respectful communication by helping you handle difficult conversations and conflicts with sensitivity. As a result, your relationships become more resilient and fulfilling.

It's important to remember that developing empathy takes time and practice. Like any skill, it requires consistent effort and a willingness to grow. Again, starting with small, everyday actions makes a huge difference. For example, making a conscious effort to listen more attentively during conversations, seeking to understand rather than immediately respond, and reflecting on your emotional experiences can all contribute to building our empathetic abilities.

Reading literature, watching films, or engaging in activities that expose you to diverse perspectives and experiences also enhances your capacity for empathy. These experiences broaden your understanding of the world and help you relate to people from different backgrounds and walks of life. Volunteering or participating in community service can provide firsthand opportunities to connect with others and practice empathy in real-life situations.

Effective Communication Techniques

Effective communication is the foundation of empathy and social skills. It allows individuals to connect on a deeper level, foster mutual understanding, and build stronger relationships. One essential aspect of effective communication is active listening. This requires you to understand the emotions and intentions behind them instead of just hearing what's being said. Active listening shows that you care about what the other person has to say, creating a sense of trust and openness in your interactions.

To practice active listening, it is important to pay full attention to the speaker. Put away distractions and maintain eye contact to show that you are engaged. Your body language should convey interest; nodding occasionally and leaning slightly forward helps signal that you are attentive. Paraphrasing or summarizing what the speaker has said demonstrates that you understand their message. For example, if someone shares a concern with you, responding with, "So, you're feeling frustrated because..." shows that you have grasped their feelings and are empathetic to their situation. Additionally, asking open-ended questions encourages further discussion and helps uncover underlying emotions. Instead of questions that elicit simple yes or no answers, try asking, "How did that make you feel?" or "What do you think might help?"

Another crucial component of effective communication is recognizing and interpreting nonverbal cues. Nonverbal communication includes facial expressions, gestures, posture, tone of voice, and even the volume at which we speak. These hints often convey more information than words alone and play a significant role in how our messages are received and understood. For instance, a smile can indicate friendliness and warmth, while crossed arms may suggest defensiveness or discomfort. Being mindful of these signals can enhance your ability to empathize with others by providing insights into their emotional states.

Using "I" statements can be particularly effective when communicating your thoughts and feelings. "I" statements allow you to express your emotions and needs without blaming others, thereby reducing misunderstandings and promoting respectful dialogue. For example, rather than saying, "You never listen to me," which can come across as accusatory, you might say, "I feel unheard when my suggestions aren't acknowledged." This approach clarifies your feelings and invites the other person to respond constructively.

Assertiveness in communication is about being clear and direct while maintaining respect for both yourself and others. It involves expressing your ideas confidently yet considerately, ensuring that your voice is heard without overshadowing those of others.

Moreover, adapting your communication style to suit the preferences of others significantly improves interpersonal connections. People have different ways of processing information and expressing themselves, so being flexible in your approach makes your interactions more effective. For example, some individuals prefer detailed explanations, while others appreciate concise summaries. Paying attention to these preferences and adjusting your communication accordingly shows empathy and consideration for the other person's needs.

Feedback is another critical element in effective communication. Being open to receiving feedback demonstrates a willingness to grow and improve, which can strengthen your relationships. Likewise, providing constructive and compassionate feedback can help others see areas where they can enhance their communication and social skills. When giving feedback, focus on specific behaviors rather than personal attributes and offer suggestions for improvement. For instance, instead of saying, "You're always late," you might say, "I've noticed that meetings often start late, which impacts our schedule. Can we find a way to ensure timely starts?" This type of feedback is more likely to be well-received and acted upon.

Building Strong Interpersonal Relationships

The foundation of healthy relationships lies in trust and respect. These two elements act as the bedrock upon which you build meaningful connections. Earning trust demands consistent behavior over time, so it requires actions that align with one's words. For example, if a friend confides in you and expects confidentiality, honoring that expectation solidifies their trust.

On the other hand, you cultivate respect by recognizing and valuing each other's boundaries. Clear boundaries help define what behaviors are acceptable and respectful within the relationship, ensuring that both parties feel safe and understood. When you communicate boundaries well, you prevent misunderstandings and create more room for mutual respect.

Nurturing relationships is an ongoing process that demands active engagement and attention. Regular check-ins play a crucial role in maintaining strong bonds, and taking the time to ask how someone is doing shows genuine interest in their well-being.

Celebrating successes together also strengthens relationships. Whether marking a promotion at work or personal milestones like birthdays, these moments of shared joy create positive memories and reinforce the connection.

Supporting each other during hardships is equally important. Offering a listening ear or a helping hand during tough times can make the people around you feel valued.

Addressing conflicts promptly is another essential aspect of nurturing relationships. Conflicts are inevitable, but how you handle them can make or break a relationship. Open communication and a willingness to understand the other person's perspective can resolve issues before they escalate.

Valuing diversity in perspectives is vital for growth and learning within relationships. Each individual brings unique experiences and viewpoints, which enrich the relationship. Embracing these differences leads to more innovative solutions and creative problem-solving. For instance, diverse viewpoints often spark new ideas in a team setting that wouldn't emerge in a homogenous group. This diversity helps individuals grow by challenging their assumptions and broadening their understanding of the world.

Creating an environment that welcomes different perspectives requires conscious effort. Open dialogue in a space where everyone feels comfortable sharing their thoughts fosters a culture of inclusivity. It's important to listen actively and acknowledge the value of each person's contributions. This approach improves the quality of your interactions and builds stronger, more resilient relationships.

Emotional resilience thrives best when supported by a solid support network, which provides a safety net during challenging times. Community participation plays a key role in this process. Being part of a community gives you a sense of belonging and access to collective resources and support. Consider engaging in community activities to build meaningful connections and develop a strong support network.

Mentorship is another powerful element in cultivating supportive relationships. A mentor provides guidance, shares wisdom from their experiences, and offers encouragement when needed. This relationship benefits both the mentor and the mentee, promoting a sense of purpose and fulfillment. Mentorship also extends beyond professional settings; it can occur in any area of life where experienced individuals guide others. For example, young professionals exploring their career paths can improve their confidence and decision-making by having a mentor who provides advice. Similarly, in personal development, a trusted mentor can help someone handle life's challenges by offering perspective and reassurance.

Teamwork and Conflict Resolution Strategies

Empathy and social skills play a crucial role in effective teamwork and conflict resolution. These interpersonal tools are essential for cultivating a collaborative environment where everyone feels valued and heard. By leveraging empathy and social skills, teams can navigate complex dynamics, overcome challenges, and achieve collective goals.

One of the fundamental aspects of successful teamwork is the ability to work together effectively. Collaborative skills are vital for group success because they bring together diverse perspectives, and that fosters creativity and innovative problem-solving. Team members with different backgrounds, experiences, and viewpoints are more likely to develop unique solutions to problems. This diversity in thinking also enhances shared accountability, as each member feels more responsible for the team's overall performance. For instance, in a project setting, a team with varied skills and knowledge can divide tasks effectively, ensuring that someone with the relevant expertise handles the corresponding aspects of the project. This approach improves performance and also builds a sense of trust and mutual respect among team members.

Open communication within teams is another critical element for resolving misunderstandings early on. Misunderstandings can quickly escalate into conflicts if not addressed promptly. Maintaining transparent and open lines of communication allows team members to express their concerns and clarify any ambiguities before they turn into bigger issues.

Clear roles and expectations also play a significant role in boosting productivity and satisfaction within a team. When everyone understands what is expected of them and their specific responsibilities, there is less room for confusion or overlap. This clarity helps keep the workflow smooth and ensures that each member contributes effectively toward the common goal.

Empathy is particularly valuable when it comes to conflict resolution. Understanding others' perspectives and acknowledging their feelings helps de-escalate tensions and pave the way for constructive dialogue. Empathetic individuals are more likely to engage in collaborative problem-solving by seeking solutions that consider everyone's needs rather than imposing their own views. Active listening is a key component of empathy, as it involves fully concentrating on the speaker, understanding their message, responding thoughtfully, and remembering what they said. It shows that you value the other person's input and are genuinely interested in finding a resolution.

It's also important to promote *psychological safety* for honest discussions within a team. Psychological safety refers to an environment where individuals feel safe to speak up without fear of retribution or embarrassment. This sense of security encourages team members to share their thoughts and ideas openly, leading to more innovative solutions and better decision-making. For example, in a brainstorming session, if team members feel psychologically safe, they are more likely to propose creative ideas without worrying about being judged. This openness can lead to breakthroughs that might not have been possible in a more restrictive atmosphere.

When conflicts arise that teams cannot resolve internally, mediation involving a neutral third party helps facilitate constructive conversations. A mediator can step in to guide the discussion and ensure that all parties have a chance to voice their concerns and work toward a mutually acceptable solution. The mediator's qualities, such as impartiality, active listening skills, and the ability to remain calm under pressure, are crucial in building trust. Trust is further enhanced when the mediator remains neutral and focused on finding a fair resolution rather than taking sides. For example, in workplace disputes, having a trained mediator helps.

In this chapter, we've discussed the importance of empathy and social skills in building and nurturing interpersonal relationships. When you try to understand cognitive and emotional empathy, you gain insight into how these skills help you connect with others on a deeper level. We've explored practical strategies such as active listening, perspective-taking, and self-reflection to improve your empathetic abilities and reduce misunderstandings.

Improving your communication techniques also plays a significant role in cultivating empathy. You can ensure more meaningful interactions through active listening, recognizing nonverbal cues, and adapting your communication styles. In doing so, you create room for personal growth and contribute to healthier and more fulfilling relationships. If you put this advice into practice, you, too, can enrich your life by creating more compassionate and resilient connections with those around you.

Chapter 5: Motivation and Self-Motivation

The only way to do great work is to love what you do. –Steve Jobs

Motivation and self-motivation are pivotal forces that drive our actions and shape our lives. To understand these concepts well, we must examine intrinsic and extrinsic motivators, which significantly influence how we approach personal and professional challenges. Intrinsic motivation refers to engaging in activities for the inherent satisfaction they provide, such as painting because it brings joy or gardening due to its therapeutic nature. On the other hand, extrinsic motivation involves performing tasks to gain external rewards like financial incentives or recognition. Balancing these two types of motivation can be complex but is essential for achieving sustained growth and fulfillment.

In this chapter, we will delve into the distinctions between intrinsic and extrinsic motivation as I share insights into how they may impact your goals and behaviors. You will find practical strategies to improve both types of motivation so they work in harmony to propel you forward. We'll also explore real-life examples to illustrate these concepts and show how individuals navigate their motivations in various scenarios. Additionally, we will discuss how understanding your motivations can lead to more meaningful goal-setting and greater resilience in the face of obstacles. This chapter aims to equip you with the tools needed to promote long-term motivation in your life.

Differences Between Intrinsic and Extrinsic Motivation

Intrinsic motivation refers to engaging in inherently rewarding activities, which promotes deep satisfaction and personal growth. We are intrinsically motivated when we do something because it brings joy or fulfillment, not because of any external reward. For example, someone might paint because they love creating art and find it therapeutic. This type of motivation often leads to higher engagement and fulfillment in tasks.

Intrinsic motivation is closely tied to our personal values and interests. When our activities align with what we genuinely care about, we are more likely to feel a sense of purpose and joy. This alignment can also enhance overall well-being. Consider the case of a person who loves gardening. They may spend hours tending to their plants, feeling a sense of peace and accomplishment as their garden flourishes. The activity itself is its own reward, cultivating both mental and emotional satisfaction.

On the other hand, extrinsic motivation involves performing tasks to earn external rewards or avoid punishments. This might include working for a paycheck, seeking praise, or trying to avoid criticism. While extrinsic motivation can be effective in driving behavior, it may not sustain long-term interest. For instance, an employee might work extra hours solely for overtime pay. Although this might boost their productivity temporarily, over time, the lack of genuine interest could lead to burnout or dissatisfaction.

The impact of these motivations on goal achievement is often significant. Recognizing whether intrinsic or extrinsic factors drive your goals helps you set more meaningful and achievable objectives. For example, if someone's primary motivation to learn a new skill is intrinsic—they enjoy the learning process and find it personally fulfilling—they are more likely to stay committed. Conversely, if they are motivated mainly by external rewards, such as recognition or financial gain, they might lose interest once those rewards are obtained or become insufficient.

Real-life examples can illustrate how different types of motivation play out in practice. I'll share a story about a successful entrepreneur, whom we'll call Maria. She started her business because she was passionate about innovative technology solutions. Her intrinsic motivation kept her going through tough times because she genuinely enjoyed the challenges and creative processes involved. In contrast, John, who entered the same industry primarily for the potential financial rewards, struggled to maintain interest and enthusiasm after his first few.

Knowing the nuances of intrinsic and extrinsic motivation can help inform your approach to professional settings. For example, companies can foster a more motivated workforce by recognizing and nurturing employees' intrinsic motivations. Allowing employees to work on projects they are passionate about, providing opportunities for personal growth, and encouraging a positive work culture can lead to sustained motivation and better performance. Conversely, while bonuses and promotions are important, relying solely on these extrinsic rewards might not yield long-term commitment or job satisfaction.

To delve deeper into practical applications, let's examine how intrinsic and extrinsic motivations influence goal-setting and commitment levels. Intrinsically motivated individuals often set goals that reflect their passions and values. These goals are usually more sustainable as they provide internal satisfaction. For example, an artist aiming to complete a series of paintings will likely stay committed because they find joy in the creative process itself.

Extrinsically motivated goals, however, might need careful consideration to ensure they are fulfilling in the long term. If an individual's goal is to achieve a certain status or income level, they should also incorporate elements that allow for personal enjoyment and satisfaction. It's crucial to balance extrinsic rewards with activities that nurture intrinsic motivations to maintain overall well-being and sustained progress.

Creating strategies for overcoming obstacles and maintaining resilience also helps to acknowledge the role of different motivations. When motivation wanes, consider reflecting on the intrinsic reasons behind your actions to encourage yourself to keep going.

Goal-Setting Techniques

When setting meaningful goals that align with intrinsic and extrinsic motivation, starting with the SMART goals framework is a valuable approach. SMART stands for specific, measurable, achievable, relevant, and time-bound, essential criteria for creating clear and focused objectives (Ogbeiwi, 2017).

Setting specific goals means being detailed about what you want to achieve. Instead of aiming to "be better at work," a specific goal would be "to complete three major projects within the next six months." This level of clarity helps you understand precisely what needs to be done and eliminates ambiguity. Specific goals serve as a roadmap, providing direction and purpose.

Measurable goals enable you to track progress and stay motivated. When you define how you will measure success, you create benchmarks that indicate your progress. For instance, if your goal is to improve fitness, measurable criteria could include tracking the number of workouts completed each week or the amount of weight lost over a specific period. These metrics provide tangible evidence of advancement, which contributes to sustained motivation.

Achievable goals are realistic and attainable, considering your current capabilities and resources. Setting too ambitious goals might lead to frustration and demotivation. Conversely, achievable goals inspire confidence and maintain momentum. It's essential to balance ambition with practicality, ensuring that your goals challenge you without becoming impossible tasks.

Relevance is critical because goals should align with broader aspirations and values. A relevant goal resonates with personal and professional priorities, making it inherently motivating. For instance, pursuing a certification that advances your career while also enhancing personal skills ensures that the effort invested is meaningful and fulfilling. Relevant goals keep you engaged by connecting day-to-day efforts to long-term desires.

Time-bound goals have deadlines, creating a sense of urgency and accountability. Setting time frames encourages consistent progress and prevents procrastination. For example, committing to read one book per month provides a structured timeline, fostering a sustained habit of learning. Time-bound goals break larger objectives into manageable segments, enhancing focus and productivity.

Visualization techniques can significantly enhance goal commitment and clarify desired outcomes. Visualization involves mentally picturing yourself achieving your goals and focusing on the positive emotions and rewards associated with success. This practice helps solidify your commitment by creating a vivid mental image of your future self. For example, visualizing a successful presentation can boost confidence and reduce anxiety, making the actual experience more manageable. Visualization acts as a rehearsal, preparing your mind for action and reinforcing your dedication to achieving your goals.

Creating an action plan is a crucial step in realizing your goals. An action plan outlines the necessary steps and timelines, breaking down larger goals into smaller, manageable tasks. This detailed road map reduces overwhelm by providing a clear path forward. For instance, if your goal is to write a book, your action plan might include daily writing targets, research sessions, and periodic reviews. An effective action plan incorporates flexibility, allowing adjustments based on progress and unforeseen challenges. Mapping out each step will enable you to transform abstract goals into actionable tasks, making the journey toward achievement more structured and less daunting.

Establishing checkpoints is vital for maintaining motivation and ensuring continuous progress. Regularly assessing your progress through established checkpoints keeps you accountable and offers opportunities for reflection and adjustment. These checkpoints act as milestones, celebrating achievements and identifying areas needing improvement. They help maintain motivation by providing frequent reminders of your progress. For example, setting monthly reviews for a long-term project allows you to evaluate what's working and what needs modification. These assessments promote a balanced perspective, ensuring that minor setbacks do not derail your overall progress. Adjustments during these checkpoints refine your approach, keeping you on track toward your ultimate goals.

Integrating the SMART goals framework can also create a comprehensive strategy for setting and achieving meaningful goals. This approach aligns both intrinsic and extrinsic motivation, giving clarity, direction, and sustained commitment. It acknowledges the importance of specificity, measurability, achievability, relevance, and time frames while emphasizing the power of mental imagery, detailed planning, and regular assessment.

The combined application of these techniques ensures that your goals are well-structured and aligned with your values and aspirations. Whether you're seeking personal growth, professional development, or a balance of both, these strategies provide the tools needed to deal effectively with the complexities of goal setting. Embracing these methods promotes a proactive approach, which empowers you to take control of your path and achieve lasting fulfillment.

Building Self-Discipline

One key pillar for sustaining both intrinsic and extrinsic motivation is developing self-discipline. Self-discipline acts as the backbone that supports your ability to stay motivated over time. You can build a solid foundation for long-term motivation when you focus on practical strategies such as establishing routines, implementing reward systems, practicing mindfulness, and finding an accountability partner.

It's essential to establish routines if you want to maintain discipline. Consistent daily routines provide structure, so they help you create a predictable environment where actions become habitual and less reliant on fleeting motivation. For example, starting your day with a set morning routine can ensure you begin with focus and purpose. This might include simple habits such as making your bed, having a healthy breakfast, and setting aside time to plan your day. These small, consistent actions help create momentum and make it easier to tackle more significant tasks throughout the day.

Reward systems are a powerful way to promote positive reinforcement. Research shows that linking our progress to rewards provides a tangible incentive to keep pushing forward (Mowbray et al., 2024). For instance, suppose you're working on a long-term project. In that case, you might set up a system where you reward yourself after reaching specific milestones, such as completing a chapter of a book or finishing a presentation. These rewards don't have to be extravagant; even small treats like enjoying a favorite snack or taking a short break can significantly impact motivation levels.

Mindfulness is another crucial aspect to consider when working to develop self-discipline. Mindfulness techniques enhance self-awareness, allowing you to notice distractions and maintain focus more effectively. Regular mindfulness practices, such as meditation or deep-breathing exercises, help calm the mind and improve concentration. For example, taking a few minutes each day to practice mindful breathing can help reset your mental state, making it easier to stay focused on tasks and avoid procrastination. Over time, these techniques can lead to better control over your thoughts and emotions, which contributes to sustained motivation.

You may also consider finding an accountability partner because having someone to share your progress with aids in maintaining discipline and commitment toward your goals. An accountability partner is someone who shares your aspirations and with whom you can regularly check in to discuss your challenges and achievements. This partnership creates a sense of social accountability, making it harder to abandon your goals when faced with challenges. For example, if you're aiming to exercise regularly, having a workout buddy can provide mutual encouragement and motivation. Knowing that someone else is invested in your success adds an extra layer of commitment, making it easier to stay on track.

Although we have covered some practical strategies that lay the groundwork for robust self-discipline, you must be flexible as you approach these strategies. Life is inherently unpredictable, and rigid adherence to routines or reward systems can sometimes lead to feelings of frustration or burnout. It's okay to adjust your strategies as needed to suit changing circumstances.

For instance, if your current routine is no longer effective due to a shift in your work schedule or personal responsibilities, take some time to reassess and create a new routine that aligns better with your current situation. Similarly, if a particular reward system starts to lose its motivational impact, consider switching up the rewards you use to keep things fresh and exciting. The goal is to balance consistency and adaptability, ensuring that your strategies remain effective over the long term.

In addition to the primary strategies we've discussed, there are complementary techniques that can further boost self-discipline and motivation. For example, journaling can be a valuable tool for tracking progress and reflecting on your journey. Writing down your goals, daily achievements, and any obstacles encountered can provide insights into what works and what needs adjustment. This practice promotes a deeper understanding of your patterns and behaviors, enabling you to make informed decisions about staying disciplined and motivated.

To sustain motivation, it's also crucial to cultivate a growth mindset. Embracing the belief that skills and abilities can be developed through effort and learning helps build resilience against setbacks. When faced with challenges, a growth mindset encourages you to view them as opportunities for growth rather than insurmountable obstacles. This perspective shift makes a significant difference in how you approach tasks and maintain your motivation over time.

Another useful technique is breaking down larger goals into smaller, manageable steps. Tackling a big project can often feel overwhelming, leading to procrastination and loss of motivation. Dividing the project into smaller tasks creates a series of achievable milestones that make the overall goal seem less daunting. Consider celebrating the completion of each step and taking in the sense of accomplishment it brings.

It's also important to surround yourself with a supportive environment. Your surroundings and the people you interact with can significantly influence your discipline and motivation. Aim to create a physical workspace that minimizes distractions and supports productivity. Additionally, seek relationships with people who inspire and encourage you to stay committed to your goals. Positive influences can act as a buffer against negative thoughts and reinforce your dedication to maintaining self-discipline.

Finally, self-compassion plays a vital role in sustaining motivation. Being kind to yourself during moments of setback or failure is essential for maintaining a healthy level of motivation. Recognize that everyone encounters obstacles, and rather than being overly critical, use these moments as learning experiences. Treat yourself with the same kindness and understanding you would offer to a friend facing similar challenges. This approach not only preserves motivation but also promotes emotional well-being.

Remember, the fundamental strategies for developing self-discipline include establishing routines, implementing reward systems, practicing mindfulness, and finding an accountability partner. Complementary techniques such as journaling, cultivating a growth mindset, breaking down goals, creating a supportive environment, and practicing self-compassion further enhance these efforts. When you integrate these strategies into your daily life, you gain the means to build a resilient foundation for long-term motivation and move closer to achieving your goals.

Sustaining Long-Term Motivation

Maintaining motivation over an extended period can be challenging, but it is crucial for personal and professional success. Let's look into some practical strategies to ensure continuous growth and adaptation:

Periodic reflection on your goals is essential to keep them relevant and aligned with your values. One effective way to do this is by scheduling regular check-ins with yourself. For instance, every month or quarter, take some time to assess whether your current objectives still resonate with your long-term aspirations. Don't hesitate to modify your goal if you find that it no longer aligns with your core values. Adjustments based on evolving circumstances ensure that your efforts remain purposeful.

Another beneficial practice is writing your goals down and placing them somewhere visible, such as a bulletin board or daily planner. This constant visual reminder keeps your objectives at the forefront of your mind, making it easier to stay committed. You might also consider using journals to document reflections on your progress. Writing about your experiences helps clarify your thoughts and offers insights into how your motivations may evolve, helping you adapt more effectively.

Developing a Growth Mindset

Cultivating a growth mindset ensures ongoing motivation through resilience and adaptability. A growth mindset is the belief that one can develop abilities and intelligence through dedication and hard work. Once you embrace this perspective, you may be able to view challenges as opportunities for growth rather than obstacles. For example, if you encounter a setback in your career, approach the situation as a learning experience instead of feeling defeated. Reflect on what went wrong and identify areas for improvement.

To promote a growth mindset, consider engaging in activities that challenge your current skills. This might include taking courses related to your field, reading books that push your understanding, or seeking feedback from peers and mentors. Active engagement with new ideas and perspectives nurtures intellectual curiosity and keeps your motivation high. You may also want to celebrate your small victories along the way. Recognizing progress, no matter how minor, reinforces the notion that effort leads to achievement.

Embracing Change

Being open to evolving interests and contexts is another key strategy for preventing stagnation. Life is dynamic, and what motivates you today may not motivate you tomorrow. Openness to change allows you to pivot when necessary, ensuring that your actions align with your current passions and external conditions.

One practical way to embrace change is to experiment with different approaches to your tasks and projects. If traditional methods feel stale, explore innovative techniques or tools that bring fresh energy to your work. It's also important to watch for new trends and developments in your field because understanding emerging practices can inspire you to adapt and stay ahead of the curve.

Networking with professionals outside your immediate circle can also expose you to diverse viewpoints and opportunities. Attending conferences, participating in online forums, and joining industry groups are excellent ways to broaden your horizons. Embracing change involves a willingness to step out of your comfort zone and seek growth in unfamiliar territories.

Building a Supportive Environment

Your environment plays a significant role in sustaining long-term motivation. Surrounding yourself with supportive and motivating influences can make a substantial difference in your ability to stay driven. Create an environment that fosters positivity and encouragement.

Start by assessing your current surroundings, both physical and social. At home and work, ensure that your spaces are organized and free of distractions. A clutter-free environment can enhance focus and productivity. On the social front, evaluate the impact of people around you. Are they uplifting and encouraging, or do they drain your energy? Strive to build a network of friends, family, and colleagues who inspire and support your goals.

Establishing routines is another practical step. Consistent daily routines form a framework for maintaining discipline. For example, start each day with a morning routine that includes setting daily intentions, which could involve meditation or planning your tasks for the day. These rituals anchor your day and provide structure that fosters sustained effort.

You can also implement reward systems to reinforce motivation. Linking progress with rewards fosters positive reinforcement. For instance, after completing a challenging project, treat yourself to something enjoyable, like a favorite meal or a day off. Rewards acknowledge your hard work, encouraging you to continue striving toward your goals.

Practicing mindfulness enhances self-awareness. Mindfulness techniques, such as meditation and deep breathing exercises, help you become more attuned to your thoughts and emotions. This heightened awareness is crucial for noticing distractions and maintaining focus on your objectives.

Finding an accountability partner can dramatically impact your motivation levels. Sharing your goals and progress with someone else provides external validation and encouragement. Whether it's a friend, family member, or colleague, having someone to share your journey with makes you more likely to stay committed. Regular check-ins with your accountability partner can keep you on track, offering mutual support and motivation.

In this chapter, we explored ways to identify and enhance intrinsic and extrinsic motivation. We delved into practical strategies for sustaining these types of motivation in various personal and professional contexts. Understanding how intrinsic motivation can lead to deep satisfaction and how extrinsic rewards can drive behavior helps set meaningful goals that align with our values and interests. Through real-life examples and detailed explanations, we saw how recognizing our motivations can influence goal commitment and overall well-being.

As you reflect on the insights gained, consider applying the discussed techniques to your life. Whether setting SMART goals, practicing mindfulness, or finding an accountability partner, these strategies can help maintain long-term motivation. Balancing intrinsic enjoyment and extrinsic rewards and remaining adaptable to change equips you to navigate challenges and stay committed to your aspirations. This thoughtful approach fosters personal growth and boosts professional success, ultimately leading to a more fulfilling and motivated life.

Chapter 6: Emotional Intelligence in Relationships

The quality of your life is in direct proportion to the quality of your relationships. –Anthony Robbins

Remember, emotional intelligence involves recognizing and managing your emotions while being attuned to the emotions of those around you. This interplay of self-awareness and empathy shapes the quality of your connections, whether personal, professional, or social. When you harness EQ, you become better equipped to improve communication and resolve conflicts more constructively while building stronger, more empathetic relationships that stand the test of time.

In this chapter, we will explore various aspects of emotional intelligence that contribute to healthier and more fulfilling relationships. We will delve into the importance of being aware of and validating your own emotions and those of others. The chapter will also cover practical techniques such as active listening and tailored communication styles, which boost empathy and understanding. Additionally, we will discuss how openly expressing emotions and recognizing nonverbal cues play a crucial role in creating an environment of trust and mutual respect. Through these insights, you will gain the tools necessary to create deeper and more meaningful connections with the people in your life.

The Role of High EQ in Forming

Connections

When learning to form meaningful connections, it's important for you to recognize and acknowledge your emotions as well as those of others. Emotional intelligence involves being aware of your feelings and understanding how they influence your thoughts and actions. Once you can recognize your own emotional state, you are better equipped to communicate effectively with others. For instance, if you're feeling frustrated or anxious, acknowledging these emotions helps you choose healthier ways to express them rather than reacting impulsively. This self-awareness minimizes misunderstandings and promotes a more transparent, honest communication style.

Equally important is the ability to recognize and validate the emotions of those around you. When you acknowledge another person's feelings, it shows that you respect their experiences and perspectives. This validation promotes a sense of empathy and connection, which is the bedrock of meaningful relationships. For example, if a friend is upset, simply acknowledging their distress and expressing empathy can significantly strengthen your bond. Showing genuine concern and understanding creates an environment that favors emotional honesty and promotes deeper connections.

High EQ individuals can express their feelings openly, which encourages intimacy and trust. Effective communication is not just about speaking; it's also about conveying your emotions in a way that builds relationships. When you can articulate your feelings openly, it allows others to see your authentic self. This openness invites reciprocity, making it easier for others to share their feelings with you. For instance, telling a partner that you appreciate their support or feel hurt by something they said opens the door for constructive dialogue. Transparency in expressing emotions eliminates guesswork and reduces potential conflicts, leading to a more resilient relationship.

Moreover, openly expressing emotions nurtures intimacy and trust, which are vital for strong bonds. Trust is built on the belief that someone will act in your best interest, which is reinforced when you consistently share your emotions honestly. When people feel trusted, they are more likely to reciprocate, creating a cycle of mutual respect and loyalty. For example, in a workplace setting, a manager who shares their challenges and asks for input demonstrates vulnerability. This approach humanizes the manager and builds a cooperative and trusting team environment.

Empathy and emotional awareness create a trustworthy environment in relationships. Empathy goes beyond mere acknowledgment of emotions to actively engaging with them. It's the capacity to share other people's feelings. When you exhibit empathy, you show that you are willing to put yourself in someone else's shoes, which is crucial for building trust. This shared understanding reassures others that their feelings are valid and important to you. For instance, when a colleague is stressed about a looming deadline, empathizing with their situation can lead to collaborative problem-solving and alleviate their stress.

Emotional awareness complements empathy by encouraging a deeper understanding of how emotions drive behaviors. When you are emotionally aware, you can better navigate interpersonal dynamics and respond appropriately to various emotional cues.

This responsiveness builds trust because it shows sensitivity to others' needs and circumstances. For example, recognizing that a friend's irritability stems from personal issues and offering support instead of reacting negatively strengthens the relationship.

Active listening demonstrates respect, reinforces connections, and increases relationship satisfaction. It involves full concentration before responding, as well as remembering the overall message. It requires putting aside distractions and focusing entirely on the speaker. This level of attentiveness conveys respect, showing that you value the other person's thoughts and feelings. When someone feels heard and understood, it enhances their sense of self-worth and trust in the relationship.

When practicing active listening, you must pay attention to nonverbal cues such as facial expressions, tone of voice, and body language. These subtle signals often convey more than the words themselves. For instance, noticing a friend's hesitance and gently encouraging them to share what's really on their mind can reveal underlying concerns that might otherwise go unaddressed. Responding thoughtfully and empathetically reinforces the connection and assures them that their feelings matter.

Additionally, active listening significantly increases relationship satisfaction (Walker et al., 2023). When both parties feel heard and understood, it lays the groundwork for effective conflict resolution and deeper emotional connections. In romantic relationships, for example, partners who practice active listening during disagreements are more likely to find mutually satisfying solutions and maintain harmony. This practice resolves issues and strengthens the relationship over time, as both individuals feel valued and respected.

Techniques for Effective and Empathetic Communication

When discussing emotional intelligence in relationships, one practical technique to encourage effective and empathetic communication is the use of "I" statements. Emphasizing personal feelings over accusations can significantly improve the quality of interactions. When individuals start their sentences with "I feel" rather than "You always," it helps articulate personal emotions without blaming the other person. For instance, saying, "I feel hurt when I am not listened to," is more constructive than "You never listen to me." This approach encourages open dialogue as it focuses on personal experiences and emotions, making the conversation less confrontational and more inviting for honest communication.

Practicing empathy is another vital aspect of leveraging emotional intelligence in relationships. Empathy involves putting oneself in another's shoes and understanding their emotions and perspectives. When empathic communication is practiced, individuals can connect on an emotional level, which helps diffuse tension and build stronger connections. In a heated discussion, pausing to say, "I can see that you're upset, and I understand why this situation is frustrating for you," can calm the atmosphere and show the other person that their feelings are acknowledged and valued. This recognition fosters mutual respect and paves the way for more peaceful interactions.

Customizing communication styles to suit the audience is crucial in enhancing receptiveness and message delivery. People vary greatly in how they process information and respond to different forms of communication. Some may prefer direct talk, while others might appreciate a more gentle and indirect approach. When you are aware of these preferences while communicating with people, you can adapt accordingly and ensure that they receive your message effectively. For example, when dealing with someone who values detailed explanations, providing thorough context behind decisions or requests can prevent misunderstandings. Conversely, keeping communication concise and to the point can be more effective for those who prefer brevity. Understanding and tailoring your communication style to meet the needs of your audience facilitates clearer and more effective exchanges.

Recognizing body language and tone of voice is also instrumental in empathetic communication. Often, nonverbal cues convey more than words themselves. A person's posture, facial expressions, and gestures can reveal underlying emotions that might not be verbally expressed. Similarly, the tone of voice—whether it is gentle, harsh, excited, or calm—can significantly impact how a message is perceived. Being attuned to these nonverbal signals allows one to respond more appropriately and empathetically. If someone is visibly anxious or upset, acknowledging their body language by saying, "You seem a bit stressed; would you like to take a moment?" can make them feel seen and understood. This kind of attentiveness contributes to better understanding and strengthens the emotional bond between individuals.

Conflict Resolution in Personal Relationships

We have established that emotional intelligence has a significant influence on how you navigate conflicts in your personal relationships. High EQ enables you to handle disagreements constructively, which fosters healthier and more resilient bonds with others.

One critical aspect of conflict resolution that high emotional intelligence facilitates is the ability to recognize emotional triggers. People often experience heightened emotions during conflicts, which can lead to escalation if not properly managed. Identifying these triggers enables individuals to take steps to calm themselves before reacting impulsively. For example, someone might notice that they feel particularly defensive when criticized. Recognizing this pattern allows them to pause, take a deep breath, and respond calmly rather than lashing out.

Creating a safe space for dialogue is another cornerstone of constructive conflict resolution. When people feel safe to express their thoughts and emotions without fear of judgment or retaliation, conversations become more focused on solutions rather than blame. High-EQ individuals are adept at creating such environments. They listen actively, validate the other person's feelings, and avoid interrupting. This encourages open communication and fosters mutual understanding. An example of this might be a couple discussing household responsibilities. Rather than accusing each other of neglecting chores, they calmly share their perspectives and work together to divide tasks fairly.

Emotional intelligence also plays a crucial role in identifying shared goals during disagreements. Often, conflicts arise because each party feels their needs or desires are misunderstood or ignored. High EQ allows individuals to step back and consider what common ground they share with the other person. For instance, two friends arguing about vacation plans may both want quality time together but have different ideas about what that looks like. Recognizing that their underlying goal is to enjoy each other's company may help them brainstorm compromises that satisfy both preferences.

Another essential element that arises from emotional intelligence is the ability to offer genuine apologies and understanding. Apologizing sincerely requires acknowledging the hurt caused and taking responsibility without excuses. Emotional intelligence helps individuals empathize with the other person's pain, making their apologies more heartfelt and effective. While this approach aids in healing wounds, it also helps rebuild trust after conflict. For example, if one partner forgot an important date, a sincere apology would involve acknowledging the impact of their forgetfulness on their partner's feelings and taking steps to ensure it doesn't happen again.

To delve deeper into these aspects, recognizing emotional triggers involves understanding one's emotional responses and the reasons behind them. Keeping a journal or engaging in self-reflection to pinpoint specific triggers is beneficial. Once you identify these triggers, you can manage them through techniques such as deep breathing, mindfulness, or even temporarily stepping away from the situation to gain clarity.

Creating a safe space for dialogue encompasses verbal communication as well as nonverbal cues. Body language, tone of voice, and facial expressions all contribute to making the other person feel heard and respected. Practicing active listening—where one focuses entirely on the speaker without planning a response—can greatly enhance the effectiveness of these conversations. It's about showing genuine interest and concern for the other person's perspective, promoting a solution-oriented mindset.

Identifying shared goals during disagreements may require asking probing questions to uncover deeper motivations and concerns. This process involves looking beyond the immediate issue to understand the broader context of the disagreement. By doing so, you may find that your goals align more closely than you initially thought. Collaborative problem-solving becomes possible, with both parties working toward mutually beneficial outcomes.

Offering genuine apologies and understanding calls for vulnerability and humility. It means setting your ego aside and focusing on restoring the relationship. A key part of this is empathetic communication, where you express understanding of the other person's feelings and experiences. Apologies should be specific, acknowledging precisely what went wrong and why it was hurtful. Follow-up actions to make amends further demonstrate sincerity and commitment to change.

Parenting With Emotional Intelligence

For parents, applying emotional intelligence greatly influences family dynamics and nurtures the children's emotional resilience. Your ability to model emotional awareness sets a foundation for your children's understanding of emotions. When you express your feelings in healthy ways, children observe and learn these behaviors. This modeling is crucial because it provides children with concrete examples of how to handle their own emotions. For instance, rather than suppressing anger or frustration, you might say, "I feel really frustrated right now because things aren't going as I planned. I need a moment to calm down." Such transparency in emotional expression demonstrates that feeling a range of emotions is normal and manageable.

Beyond verbalizing feelings, you may also consider displaying nonverbal cues associated with your emotions to teach your children the full spectrum of emotional communication. When you are visibly happy, sad, or anxious, acknowledging these feelings helps children recognize and understand similar emotions within themselves. This modeling also teaches them appropriate responses following their parent's observable behavior.

Creating an environment supportive of emotional expression is vital for children's emotional development. Children thrive in settings where they feel safe expressing their feelings without judgment or reprimand. You can foster such an environment by actively listening to your children and validating their emotions. For example, if a child comes home upset after a difficult day at school, as a high-EQ parent, you might say, "It sounds like you had a tough day. Do you want to talk about what happened?" This approach assures the child that their feelings are important, valued, and worthy of attention.

Furthermore, establishing routines that encourage open dialogue about emotions greatly contributes to your children's comfort in expressing feelings. Family discussions about daily highs and lows or creating "emotion charts" where children can visually represent their feelings are effective strategies. These practices normalize emotional sharing and reduce stigma around expressing vulnerability, fostering a more emotionally intelligent household.

High EQ parents play a critical role in guiding children through conflict resolution and teaching them empathy during disputes. Handling conflicts calmly and constructively gives your children a blueprint for resolving their own disagreements. In situations of sibling rivalry, for instance, you can mediate by encouraging each child to share their perspective while actively listening to the other. This approach resolves the immediate conflict and instills essential skills for peaceful dispute resolution.

Moreover, you can teach empathy by asking questions that prompt your children to consider others' feelings. During a conflict, you may ask, "How do you think your brother felt when you took his toy?" Such questions help children develop the ability to see situations from another person's perspective, which is an essential component of empathy. Regularly practicing this technique encourages your children to approach conflicts with a mindset geared toward understanding and resolution rather than blame and anger.

Acknowledging each child's unique emotional needs allows you to tailor your parenting approaches, which strengthens the parent-child bond. Every child experiences and processes emotions differently; some may be more sensitive, while others might be more reserved. As a high EQ parent, you can try to understand these individual differences and adapt their methods accordingly. For instance, a child who tends to internalize stress may benefit from more one-on-one time with a parent to talk through their worries. In contrast, a more expressive child might appreciate joint physical activities to release pent-up energy.

Understanding these differences enables you to support your children in ways that resonate most effectively with them. This personalized attention boosts their sense of security and trust within the family dynamic. It also fosters a deeper connection as they feel understood and valued for who they truly are.

Emotional intelligence significantly enhances your relationships by fostering deeper connections and understanding. In this chapter, we've explored the importance of recognizing and acknowledging your own emotions and those of others. This self-awareness helps in expressing feelings openly and choosing healthier ways to communicate, which minimizes misunderstandings and promotes honesty. Validating others' emotions shows respect for their experiences, creating an empathetic environment that welcomes emotional honesty and strengthens bonds.

Furthermore, active listening and empathy are pivotal in building trust and satisfaction within relationships. When you fully concentrate on what others are saying and put distractions aside, you convey respect and value for their thoughts and feelings. Tailoring your communication styles to suit different audiences, recognizing body language, and offering genuine apologies all constructively resolve conflicts. These techniques help you nurture trust, intimacy, and mutual respect, ultimately improving the quality of your interactions and making your relationships more resilient.

Chapter 7: Applying Emotional Intelligence at Work

The greatest ability in business is to get along with others and influence their actions. –John Hancock

Applying emotional intelligence at work involves understanding and managing both your own emotions and those of others to create a peaceful workplace. This skill extends beyond mere awareness of feelings, encompassing the ability to navigate complex social interactions, resolve conflicts amicably, and build strong professional relationships. In a diverse and dynamic work environment, emotional intelligence can be the key to mastering better communication, greater empathy, and higher resilience among team members. Actively applying EQ principles enables professionals to improve their performance and positively influences the morale and productivity of their colleagues.

In this chapter, we will explore various aspects of emotional intelligence and how you can practically apply them in professional settings. You'll learn about the importance of emotional self-awareness and regulation and how these skills can enhance your job performance. We will discuss techniques for improving interpersonal relationships, from networking effectively to fostering collaboration within teams. You'll also discover strategies for balancing assertiveness with empathy, which is crucial for healthy professional interactions. By the end of this chapter, you will have gained a comprehensive understanding of how emotional intelligence can transform your work environment and contribute to your overall career success.

The Importance of EQ in Professional Success

In today's competitive job market, emotional intelligence is a key differentiator for professionals seeking to stand out. Remember, unlike IQ, which measures cognitive abilities, EQ encompasses the ability to understand and manage one's own emotions and those of others. This skill is invaluable as it influences how we navigate social complexities, build relationships, and make decisions. For instance, during job interviews, candidates with high EQ often exhibit better self-awareness and articulate their experiences more effectively, making a lasting impression on potential employers.

Moreover, emotional intelligence plays a pivotal role in job performance. Employees with high emotional intelligence are generally better at managing stress, communicating effectively, and resolving conflicts amicably (Yamani et al., 2014). For example, a project manager with strong EQ will be adept at recognizing team members' emotional states and addressing them proactively, thus maintaining a harmonious work environment. This enhances individual productivity and contributes to overall team performance, both of which drive success for the organization.

Adaptability and resilience are other crucial areas where EQ proves beneficial. In any professional setting, change is inevitable, whether it's adopting new technologies, adjusting to restructured teams, or dealing with economic fluctuations. Individuals with high EQ are typically more adaptable; they can adjust their thinking and behavior to suit evolving circumstances. Resilience, a key component of emotional intelligence, empowers professionals to recover from setbacks and persist through challenges. For example, during a corporate merger, employees with strong emotional intelligence can better manage their anxieties, foster cooperation among colleagues, and adapt to new corporate cultures more smoothly.

Leadership effectiveness is intrinsically linked to emotional intelligence. Leaders with high EQ are often more effective because they inspire trust, communicate vision clearly, and foster an environment of motivation. They understand that leading a team isn't just about issuing directives but also about connecting with team members on a personal level. Such leaders are great at recognizing the strengths and weaknesses of their team, providing support where needed, and motivating individuals to perform at their best. An emotionally intelligent leader, for instance, might recognize when a team member is feeling overwhelmed and offer encouragement or practical solutions to help alleviate their stress, thus promoting a positive work environment and enhancing overall team performance.

Understanding emotions contributes to better job performance by enabling professionals to navigate interpersonal relations more effectively. When employees are good at recognizing and interpreting their own emotions and those of their colleagues, they can respond more appropriately in various situations. This leads to better teamwork, reduced conflicts, and enhanced collaboration. For example, a salesperson with high emotional intelligence can gauge a client's mood and adjust their sales pitch accordingly, increasing the likelihood of closing a deal.

Similarly, high EQ makes dealing with change and promoting adaptability more manageable. Professionals equipped with these skills are more likely to embrace new challenges and view them as opportunities for growth rather than threats. This mindset aids in personal development and also contributes to organizational resilience. During times of transition, such as implementing a new company-wide software system, employees with high emotional intelligence can lead by example by showing their peers how to adopt new processes seamlessly and maintain productivity.

Emotional intelligence also improves leadership. Leaders with high EQ become mentors and coaches who can identify and nurture talent within their teams. They create a supportive atmosphere that encourages open communication and constructive feedback. This approach promotes continuous learning and development, contributing to individual career growth and organizational success. For instance, a leader who regularly checks in with team members and offers personalized feedback helps create a culture of continuous improvement and engagement.

Building Strong Professional Relationships

In today's rapidly evolving professional environment, emotional intelligence is a critical factor in establishing and maintaining productive professional relationships. Understanding and applying EQ at work significantly improves one's ability to network, collaborate, and build trust. Let's delve into these aspects to understand how they contribute to a thriving workplace.

Networking for Career Development

Networking is a vital skill in any professional setting. It involves forming and nurturing relationships that can help in career growth and development. Emotional intelligence plays a crucial role here because when you are emotionally intelligent, you can understand and manage your own emotions, as well as those of others. This awareness helps you handle social situations more effectively.

To refine your networking skills, it's important to genuinely connect with people. Individuals with high EQ can empathize with others, fostering meaningful interactions. Instead of seeing networking merely as a transactional activity, someone with high EQ considers it building long-term relationships based on mutual respect and understanding. This approach often leads to more fruitful and lasting connections.

Active listening, an essential component of EQ, also improves networking abilities. Calmly listening to what others have to say without planning your response while they are speaking shows that you value their input and perspective. This creates a positive impression and encourages open and honest communication.

To improve your networking skills, practice active listening and make an effort to understand the emotions behind the words. Show genuine interest in others' experiences and perspectives, and seek to build authentic connections rather than just professional contacts.

Nurturing Teamwork

Collaboration is at the heart of any successful team. High emotional intelligence facilitates better teamwork by fostering an environment where all team members feel valued and understood. When team members have high EQ, they can easily recognize and respect each other's emotional states, leading to smoother interactions and less conflict.

A team with high collective EQ can more effectively handle both successes and setbacks. They celebrate wins together and support each other through challenges. This emotional awareness and mutual support create a collaborative workspace where creativity and productivity thrive.

Moreover, leaders with high EQ can connect with their team members on a deeper level, understanding their needs and motivations. This connection enables them to guide their teams more effectively, ensuring everyone is aligned toward common goals.

Encourage open communication and create a safe space for team members to express their thoughts and feelings. Recognize and validate each person's contributions and use empathetic leadership to foster a supportive team culture.

Balancing Assertiveness and Empathy

Assertiveness involves standing up for oneself and expressing one's needs clearly, whereas empathy involves understanding and valuing the feelings and perspectives of others. High-EQ individuals can strike this balance effectively, which means they can express their voices without overshadowing others.

In professional settings, an imbalance between assertiveness and empathy can lead to misunderstandings and conflicts. If one is too assertive, it may come off as aggressive; if too empathetic, one might be perceived as passive. Finding the right balance means being able to communicate one's needs and boundaries while also being receptive and responsive to others.

Practicing this balance involves being mindful during interactions. Before responding, consider the emotional impact your words will have on others. It's about being firm yet kind, direct yet considerate. This equilibrium helps build stronger professional relationships where mutual respect and cooperation are paramount.

To balance assertiveness and empathy, take time to reflect before responding during interactions. Aim to express your needs clearly while considering and respecting the emotions and perspectives of others. This balanced approach will lead to healthier and more effective professional communications.

Trust and Respect

Finally, trust and respect form the foundation of any productive professional relationship. Emotional intelligence is key to developing these attributes. Approaching your colleagues with empathy, understanding, and respect naturally builds trust.

Trust develops over time through consistent behavior, so you must be reliable, keep your promises, and show integrity in all your actions. A person with high EQ is mindful of their behavior and understands its impact on their relationships. They strive to maintain a positive attitude, even in challenging situations, which reassures their colleagues and builds trust.

Respect goes hand in hand with trust. It involves recognizing and valuing the unique strengths and contributions of each individual. In a workplace where respect is prevalent, diversity of thought and experience is celebrated, and everyone feels included.

Conflict Resolution at Work

Understanding emotions in conflict is the cornerstone of effectively navigating workplace disagreements. Emotions often run high in conflicts, making recognizing and understanding these emotional states essential. When individuals acknowledge their own feelings and those of their colleagues, they create a foundation for empathetic communication. For instance, frustration and anxiety might surface when a project deadline is missed. Identifying these emotions enables you to address the root cause of the conflict rather than just the symptoms. This understanding sets the stage for resolution by promoting a more constructive dialogue.

Active listening techniques are integral to improving conflict resolution effectiveness. When two team members disagree on a project approach, active listening can help each party feel heard and valued. This de-escalates tension and also paves the way for a collaborative solution. Encouraging phrases like "I understand why you feel this way" or "Can you tell me more about your concerns?" show empathy and contribute to a more peaceful workplace environment.

Mediating with empathy plays a critical role in finding common ground during workplace conflicts. Empathy involves putting oneself in another's shoes and genuinely trying to understand their emotions and viewpoints. This practice helps bridge gaps and create a more compassionate discourse. For example, if a conflict arises from perceived unfair workload distribution, acknowledging the feelings of stress and resentment allows for a more empathetic discussion. Mediators who employ empathy can facilitate conversations where both parties feel respected and understood. This empathetic approach often leads to mutually acceptable solutions and strengthens professional relationships.

A problem-solving approach that uses emotional insights can significantly enhance collaborative efforts in resolving conflicts. Emotional intelligence provides valuable insights into not just the issue at hand but also the underlying emotional dynamics. For example, when tackling a conflict over resource allocation, understanding that one team's urgency might stem from client pressure while another's resistance might be due to existing workload can help tailor a more effective solution. Acknowledging these emotional dimensions enables teams to brainstorm and focus on solutions that respect everyone's needs and constraints. Approaching problems with an emotionally intelligent mindset encourages open communication and creative problem-solving.

Integrating these principles requires ongoing commitment and practice. For instance, regularly scheduled workshops on emotional intelligence and conflict resolution can equip employees with the necessary skills and knowledge. Role-playing exercises allow participants to practice recognizing emotions, active listening, and empathetic mediation in a controlled, supportive setting. These activities can make emotional intelligence second nature, ensuring it becomes a part of the organizational culture.

Motivating and Inspiring Teams

Emotional intelligence has become a cornerstone of modern leadership, particularly when it comes to motivating and inspiring team members. One primary way to achieve this is by creating a positive emotional climate within the workplace. An emotionally intelligent leader understands that emotions are contagious and that their own behavior can significantly influence the mood and atmosphere of the entire team. Leaders can create an inclusive environment by maintaining a positive, enthusiastic demeanor.

For instance, a manager who starts each meeting with encouraging words and acknowledges team members' hard work sets a positive tone and motivates people to bring their best selves to work. Creating a positive emotional climate involves more than occasional praise; it requires consistent effort to show empathy, provide constructive feedback, and foster an inclusive atmosphere where everyone feels heard and appreciated.

Empowering team members is another crucial aspect of leveraging emotional intelligence in the workplace. When team members feel empowered, they are more likely to take initiative and contribute meaningfully towards shared goals. Emotional intelligence enables leaders to recognize individual strengths and opportunities for growth within the team. Leaders can inspire confidence and boost morale by delegating tasks that align with each member's abilities and giving them the autonomy to execute these tasks.

One practical example of this empowerment is through participative decision-making. Engaging team members in discussions about strategies, goals, and processes makes them feel responsible for the outcomes and more committed to achieving them. Regularly seeking input and genuinely considering their advice can make a profound impact on their motivation levels. Providing opportunities for professional development, such as training or mentorship programs, further empowers individuals to reach their full potential.

Searching for intrinsic motivators is another powerful way that emotional intelligence can drive team success. Unlike extrinsic motivators, such as bonuses or promotions, intrinsic motivators are internal desires that propel individuals to take action because they find the activity itself rewarding. Emotional intelligence helps leaders identify what truly inspires their team members by tuning into their unique interests, values, and goals.

If you are a leader, you can consider having one-on-one meetings with team members to discuss their personal aspirations and how their current roles can align with these goals. When you know what drives each person, you can tailor your approach to ensure that projects and tasks resonate on a deeper level. For example, if a team member is passionate about environmental sustainability, you may assign them to a project that addresses eco-friendly practices within the company. This alignment boosts job satisfaction and also fosters long-term commitment.

Sustained motivation is critical for continuous progress and achievement. Emotional intelligence techniques, such as encouragement and support, play a vital role in maintaining high levels of motivation over time. It's easy to feel motivated at the start of a new project, but sustaining that motivation through challenges and setbacks requires ongoing effort from the leader.

One effective approach is to celebrate small wins along the way. Breaking down larger goals into smaller, manageable milestones allows for frequent recognition and celebration of progress. This keeps the team's energy high and provides a sense of accomplishment, making the ultimate goal seem more attainable. Offering emotional support during challenging times by actively listening and showing understanding also helps team members navigate stress and remain focused.

Another technique involves promoting a culture of open communication where team members feel safe to express their thoughts and concerns without fear of judgment. Regular check-ins and feedback sessions ensure that you address any issues promptly, which encourages persistence and prevents negative emotions from building up.

This chapter has highlighted the vital role of emotional intelligence in professional settings, focusing on how it improves workplace dynamics and promotes a productive atmosphere. You can improve communication, reduce conflicts, and promote strong working relationships by understanding and managing emotions—both your own and those of others. These skills also contribute to long-term professional success because EQ enables you to connect more authentically and work more harmoniously with colleagues.

Emotionally intelligent leaders also play a crucial role in inspiring and motivating their teams. Creating a positive emotional climate and empowering team members enables you to set the stage for continuous growth and achievement as you nurture your team.

Chapter 8: Emotional Intelligence for Personal Growth

Your emotions are the slaves to your thoughts, and you are the slave to your emotions. –Elizabeth Gilbert

Emotional intelligence is essential for personal growth as it plays a crucial role in how we understand and manage our emotions to improve our lives. As we journey through self-improvement, boosting our emotional intelligence builds resilience and also makes us more adaptable to the changes we encounter in life. Embracing this aspect of personal development allows us to know ourselves better and confront challenges positively.

In this chapter, we will explore various facets of emotional intelligence and its impact on continuous self-improvement. We'll explore the significance of emotional intelligence in fostering resilience to make you more adaptable. Examining practical strategies and techniques, such as identifying core values, setting SMART goals, tracking progress, overcoming obstacles, and integrating mindfulness practices, gives you valuable insights into how you can harness emotional intelligence for personal growth. This holistic approach aims to provide you with the tools you need to develop emotional resilience and better navigate interpersonal relationships.

Setting and Achieving Personal Goals

Your core values are an essential aspect of personal goal-setting. These are the principles or standards you hold most dear and deeply influence your behavior and decisions. Exploring these values enables you to align your goals with what truly matters to you. This alignment creates a sense of purpose and direction, which makes your objectives more meaningful and rewarding. For example, if one of your core values is family, setting a goal to spend more quality time with loved ones can be far more motivating than a goal unrelated to your personal aspirations.

Reflecting on your core values can lead to significant insights about your motivations and priorities. Journaling or discussing your values with trusted friends or mentors can help clarify what truly drives you. An individual who values creativity might set goals related to artistic pursuits, while someone who prioritizes health may focus on fitness and nutrition. This value-based approach ensures that your goals are not just arbitrary tasks but reflections of your deeper self.

Once you've identified your core values, the next step is to apply the SMART criteria to your goal-setting process to ensure clear and achievable goals. SMART stands for specific, measurable, achievable, relevant, and time-bound.

Consider the goal of improving physical fitness. A general goal might be, "I want to get in shape." However, a SMART goal would transform this into specific steps: "I will run three times a week for 30 minutes each session and aim to complete a 5K race in three months." This goal is specific (running), measurable (three times a week, 30 minutes per session), achievable (based on current fitness level), relevant (aligned with the value of health), and time-bound (three months).

Breaking down larger goals into smaller, manageable steps makes them less intimidating and more actionable. For instance, if your broader goal is to write a book, breaking it down into smaller tasks, such as "write 500 words a day," can make the overall process feel more achievable and keep you motivated by providing regular milestones to celebrate.

Monitoring your progress is crucial in maintaining motivation and ensuring you remain on track to achieve your goals. Regular reviews allow you to reflect on what's working well and identify areas for improvement. This process helps maintain momentum and allows you to adjust your strategies as necessary.

Consider using tools such as journals, apps, or simple spreadsheets to log your daily or weekly progress. Reflect on both your successes and the challenges you encounter. For example, if your goal is to save money, tracking your expenses and savings can highlight spending habits that need adjustment. Celebrating small wins along the way, like saving a certain amount each month, can boost your morale and encourage further effort.

In addition to self-monitoring, seeking feedback from others can provide valuable perspectives and keep you accountable. You may also share your progress with a mentor or peer group for encouragement and constructive criticism, both of which enrich your journey toward achieving your goals.

Overcoming Obstacles

Achieving significant goals often involves facing various obstacles. It's essential that you develop strategies to overcome these barriers for long-term success and resilience. Remember, challenges are a natural part of any journey, and approaching them with a problem-solving mindset can turn potential setbacks into opportunities for growth.

Start by identifying potential obstacles that could impede your progress. This awareness allows you to prepare and strategize effectively. For example, if time management is a challenge, creating a detailed schedule and prioritizing tasks may help mitigate this issue. If motivation wanes, finding ways to reignite your passion—such as revisiting your core values or seeking inspiration from others—can be beneficial.

Embracing challenges as learning opportunities strengthens your resilience. Instead of viewing failures as negative outcomes, try to see them as feedback and give yourself a chance to refine your approach. For instance, if you miss a workout session, analyze what caused the lapse and adjust your plan to prevent future occurrences. This proactive mindset fosters continuous improvement and perseverance.

Moreover, cultivating a support network provides emotional and practical assistance when facing obstacles. Friends, family, coaches, or support groups can offer advice and help you stay motivated, even during tough times.

The Role of Mindfulness in Personal Growth

As you may remember, mindfulness is the practice of deliberately focusing your attention on the present moment without judgment. It requires you to be fully aware of your environment, feelings, thoughts, and sensations. This simple concept plays a critical role in emotional intelligence by promoting self-awareness. When you are mindful, you gain a clearer understanding of your emotions and can respond to situations with intention rather than reacting impulsively. This shift from reaction to intentionality can significantly improve your emotional regulation and personal interactions.

Mindfulness Techniques

There are various mindfulness techniques that you can adopt based on your preferences. One popular method is mindful breathing, which involves paying close attention to your breath as it flows in and out. This technique can be practiced anywhere and helps anchor the mind, reducing stress and increasing focus. Another valuable technique is meditation. Whether it's guided or unguided, meditation provides a structured way to cultivate mindfulness over time. You may also use body scans to mentally scan through different parts of your body while noting any sensations. These can also promote relaxation and heighten bodily awareness.

It's essential to find the technique that resonates most with you. In the beginning, consider engaging for a few minutes each day. That way, you can gradually practice for longer as you become more comfortable. Incorporating these practices into your daily routine makes mindfulness more accessible and sustainable.

Integrating Mindfulness Into Daily Life

Weaving mindfulness into everyday activities can be a game-changer for improving present-moment awareness. Simple strategies, such as mindful eating, involve savoring each bite and noticing the flavors, textures, and aromas of your food. This enhances the sensory experience and aids in better digestion and appreciation of meals. Similarly, practicing mindfulness during mundane tasks such as washing dishes or taking a shower can change these routines into opportunities for mental clarity and calmness.

You can start by choosing one everyday activity to practice mindfulness each day. Then, pay full attention to the task at hand without letting your mind wander. Over time, this habit will help you stay grounded and promote a greater sense of presence throughout your day.

Benefits for Personal Growth

The practice of mindfulness has far-reaching impacts on personal and emotional development. Regular mindfulness exercises can lead to greater emotional stability and help individuals navigate life's ups and downs with more resilience. Mindfulness boosts self-awareness, allowing you to better recognize and understand your emotional triggers. This heightened awareness promotes healthier responses and reduces the likelihood of emotional outbursts.

Moreover, mindfulness helps develop empathy and compassion, both toward oneself and others. Being attuned to the present moment enables you to become more sensitive to the needs and emotions of those around you. This empathetic approach can improve relationships and foster deeper connections with others. Self-compassion, an integral aspect of mindfulness, also encourages a kind and forgiving attitude toward oneself, especially during challenging times. This self-care mindset is essential for long-term personal growth and well-being.

Mindfulness practices also contribute to cognitive improvements. Studies indicate that regular mindfulness meditation boosts concentration, memory, and problem-solving skills (Sevinc et al., 2021). These cognitive benefits are invaluable for personal and professional development, which enables individuals to perform better in various aspects of their lives.

Practices for Boosting Self-Discipline

Self-discipline is crucial when working toward personal growth and goal achievement. Before proceeding, you must understand and integrate several key techniques into your daily lives.

The Power of Routines and Setting Boundaries

Establishing daily routines promotes discipline and consistency. When you create a structured schedule, you can reinforce good habits until they become second nature. For instance, starting the day with rituals like morning exercise, meditation, or reading creates a stable foundation that positively influences the rest of the day. These routines help keep you on track and minimize the decisions you need to make, thus conserving mental energy for more important tasks. Developing these habits might feel challenging initially, but over time, they promote a sense of order and predictability that can be incredibly empowering.

Another cornerstone of self-discipline is the establishment of clear personal boundaries. Boundaries are essential in maintaining focus and reducing distractions. For example, setting specific times for work and leisure can prevent the blurring of lines between professional responsibilities and personal time. Communicating these boundaries to others is also beneficial in managing their expectations effectively. This way, you can protect your time and energy from being consumed by external demands that could derail your progress. Practicing saying no when necessary is a powerful tool in upholding these boundaries, ensuring that you prioritize what truly matters to you without feeling guilty.

Accountability Partnerships and Using Incentives

Incorporating incentives into your routine greatly enhances motivation and discipline. Rewards serve as tangible acknowledgments of your efforts, making it easier to stay committed to your goals. For instance, rewarding yourself with a favorite treat after completing a difficult task or taking a short break after an hour of focused work can boost morale and productivity. The key is to celebrate small victories along the way, which helps maintain momentum and encourages continued effort. Over time, anticipating these rewards can transform challenging activities into more enjoyable experiences, fostering a positive cycle of motivation and accomplishment.

Sharing your goals with others can significantly boost self-discipline through accountability partnerships. Having someone to share your successes and setbacks with creates a sense of responsibility and commitment. These partnerships can involve regular check-ins where you update each other on your progress, discuss challenges, and offer support. Such interactions can deepen relationships and provide a source of external motivation. Knowing that someone else is invested in your success can drive you to stay disciplined and persevere even when faced with obstacles.

Creating and Maintaining a Balanced Life

Finding balance in life is vital for overall well-being and happiness. A balanced life allows you to effectively deal with the complex demands of work, relationships, and self-care, contributing significantly to emotional resilience and personal growth. Let's delve into the importance of achieving this balance and the methods for doing so.

Your first step toward achieving a peaceful life is understanding the key areas that require balance. These areas often include work, relationships, and self-care. After you recognize which aspects dominate your time and energy, you can then identify where adjustments are necessary.

For example, someone who is overly focused on their career might find that their personal relationships or self-care routines suffer as a result. Similarly, a person who devotes a significant amount of time to social activities may neglect professional responsibilities or personal health. Taking a moment to assess these areas helps to highlight imbalances.

Time Management Techniques

Effective time management plays a pivotal role in maintaining balance. Practical tools such as calendars and planners help organize tasks and allocate time appropriately. These tools enable individuals to schedule their work commitments, personal activities, and self-care routines systematically.

For instance, setting specific times for work tasks, breaks, family time, and exercise can ensure that no single area consumes all available time. Tools like digital calendars also provide reminders for important activities, helping to keep tasks on track and reduce the stress associated with last-minute rushes.

Creating to-do lists further improves time management. By prioritizing tasks based on urgency and importance, you can focus on tasks that need immediate attention while still making room for less critical activities. This method prevents overwhelming feelings and promotes productivity.

Regular Reflection for Balance

It's important to implement regular check-ins to assess life balance and well-being. Practices such as journaling or conducting self-assessments can help you reflect on your current state and recognize any imbalance. These reflections serve as a tool to spot stress points and areas needing improvement.

Journaling, for example, allows you to document daily experiences, thoughts, and emotions. This practice helps reveal patterns over time, so it indicates if you are consistently neglecting certain areas. Self-assessments, on the other hand, involve evaluating one's satisfaction with various life domains, such as career, relationships, and personal development.

Setting aside time for weekly or monthly reflections can be particularly beneficial. During these sessions, you can review your accomplishments and any challenges you may have faced. You can then adjust accordingly to ensure sustained well-being.

Self-Care Practices

We often overlook self-care, but it's a fundamental component in maintaining balance. It involves dedicating time and effort to activities that promote physical, mental, and emotional health. Prioritizing self-care promotes resilience and prevents burnout, enabling us to handle life's demands more effectively.

Physical self-care includes regular exercise, sufficient sleep, and nutritious eating habits. Engaging in physical activities improves your overall health and also reduces stress levels. It's also important to ensure adequate sleep, as it allows your body and mind to rejuvenate.

Mental self-care involves participating in activities that stimulate your mind and reduce stress. Some examples include reading, solving puzzles, or learning new skills. Emotional self-care focuses on identifying and expressing feelings in a healthy manner. Practices such as meditation, mindfulness, and spending time on hobbies all contribute to better emotional well-being.

Social self-care emphasizes the importance of building and maintaining supportive relationships. You can practice this by spending quality time with your loved ones, participating in social groups, or maintaining regular communication with friends and family, which can enhance a sense of connectedness and support.

To integrate self-care practices into your daily life, you can create routines that incorporate small but consistent self-care activities. For instance, you can start the day with a short meditation session, take periodic breaks during work to stretch or walk, and then end the day with a relaxing activity, such as reading or a warm bath.

We have covered the significance of setting and achieving personal goals by understanding core values, using the SMART goals framework, and integrating mindfulness practices. As you put these into practice, you'll appreciate that aligning your goals with what truly matters creates a purposeful direction that boots motivation. Using tools like journaling and regular progress reviews helps you maintain clarity and momentum, which ensures your efforts are effective and rewarding. Embracing challenges with a problem-solving mindset also promotes resilience and continuous improvement, both of which make you better equipped to handle setbacks.

Maintaining balance through effective time management, self-care, and establishing boundaries is essential for sustaining progress toward your goals. Mindfulness enriches your emotional intelligence while promoting adaptability. Weaving these principles into your daily life boosts your ability to manage stress and improve relationships. Ultimately, the journey of self-improvement through emotional intelligence cultivates a resilient and adaptable mindset that promotes overall well-being and personal growth.

Chapter 9: Building a Supportive Emotional Environment

When working on personal and collective growth, it's crucial that you build a supportive emotional environment. The essence of such a system lies in creating connections that nurture emotional intelligence and provide a sense of belonging. Your relationships are the foundation of your emotional resilience, allowing you to navigate life's challenges with reduced stress and increased motivation. Establishing strong, supportive bonds within your immediate communities—be it workplaces, social groups, or local centers—can significantly enhance our psychological well-being. Encouraging these connections broadens your perspective and enriches your life with mutual encouragement and diverse viewpoints.

This chapter explores practical strategies for cultivating these essential connections within familiar circles and through external networks. It emphasizes the importance of actively engaging in community activities and leveraging digital platforms to form meaningful relationships beyond geographical limitations. We will explore the significance of maintaining these bonds through regular check-ins, shared experiences, and intentional efforts to foster vulnerability and trust. When you understand the value of authentic interactions and the role of consistent, positive reinforcement, you gain insights into building a supportive environment that promotes resilience.

Developing Supportive Networks

Building a supportive emotional environment is pivotal for personal and collective growth. One of the foremost aspects is creating connections that nurture emotional growth and provide a sense of belonging. Your relationships form the bedrock of emotional resilience, and establishing solid and supportive bonds with those around you can significantly reduce stress levels (Hostinar & Gunnar, 2015). When facing challenges, having access to diverse perspectives broadens your outlook and motivates you to persevere.

Creating these connections often begins by looking within communities you are already part of, such as workplaces, social groups, or even local community centers. Attending events and participating in group activities can naturally lead to forming new relationships. However, it is equally important to recognize the potential of external networks. For instance, leveraging social media platforms and attending workshops or webinars can help forge meaningful connections beyond geographical constraints.

Networking strategies are essential tools in building these relationships. In today's digital age, social media platforms like LinkedIn, Facebook, and Twitter provide ample opportunities for connecting with like-minded individuals. These platforms allow us to join groups and forums where we can share ideas, seek advice, and offer support. Online workshops and seminars also present another avenue to meet people who share similar interests and goals, thus expanding our network in ways previously unimaginable.

However, being mindful and intentional about the connections you make on these platforms is essential. Engaging actively and meaningfully rather than passively consuming content makes a significant difference. It's wise to view networking as an opportunity to build genuine relationships rather than thinking of it merely as a way to increase contacts.

Maintaining these relationships requires effort and consistency. Consider using regular check-ins, such as phone calls, messages, or face-to-face meetings, to strengthen relational ties. The sessions don't always have to be lengthy or formal interactions; sometimes, a short message just to see how someone is doing can go a long way. Shared experiences, such as joint projects or collaborative efforts, further cement these bonds.

Planning regular meet-ups or reunions also helps reinvigorate connections that may have waned over time. Even virtual gatherings, such as video calls or online games, may help maintain a sense of closeness. Creating traditions, such as annual get-togethers or monthly discussion groups, also helps sustain these relationships over the long term.

The role of vulnerability in building supportive networks cannot be overstated. Sharing personal experiences, including struggles and challenges, promotes deeper understanding and trust among individuals. When you open up about your vulnerabilities, you invite others to do the same, creating a safe space for genuine interactions. This authenticity helps attract like-minded individuals who appreciate and empathize with your experiences, contributing to stronger and more meaningful connections.

Vulnerability serves as a bridge between superficial interactions and deep, lasting relationships. It allows you to connect with others on a human level, reminding you that everyone faces difficulties and that it's okay to seek support. Moreover, being vulnerable can lead to personal growth, as it often requires courage and reflection. Acknowledging and sharing your weaknesses with others enables you to work toward overcoming them together.

However, it is important to gauge the appropriate level of vulnerability in different contexts. Not every setting or relationship is conducive to sharing deeply personal experiences immediately. Building trust gradually and ensuring a supportive environment before delving into more intimate topics can prevent discomfort and misunderstandings. You may start by sharing smaller, less intense experiences and observing the responses and level of empathy from others. Over time, as you establish mutual trust, you may share more significant experiences and further deepen the bond.

Creating Positive Emotional Climates

Creating a supportive emotional environment is essential for fostering personal and mutual growth. You can achieve this through various methods that encourage positive interactions and emotional wellness. One of the foundational steps in this process is establishing ground rules. When guidelines for interaction are clear, they create safe spaces for open dialogue and minimize misunderstandings. For instance, setting expectations around respectful communication, active listening, and confidentiality helps individuals feel secure in expressing their thoughts and feelings. Such ground rules ensure that discussions remain constructive and everyone's voice is heard, promoting a sense of trust and respect within the group.

In addition to establishing ground rules, it's crucial to encourage positivity within the environment. Regularly expressing appreciation and celebrating wins enhances morale and camaraderie among participants. Simple gestures like acknowledging someone's effort or celebrating small milestones can significantly boost the collective spirit. Positive reinforcement promotes a culture where individuals feel valued and motivated to contribute their best. For example, a team leader who consistently recognizes achievements, both big and small, nurtures an atmosphere of encouragement and support. This improves individual well-being and also strengthens the overall cohesiveness of the group.

Feedback mechanisms play a vital role in maintaining a supportive emotional environment. Implementing structured feedback sessions and anonymous forms encourages constructive feedback and openness without fear of judgment. By providing regular opportunities for feedback, you can express your concerns and suggestions, which leads to continuous improvement. Structured feedback sessions allow for reflective dialogue, where you can share your experiences and receive thoughtful responses. On the other hand, Anonymous forms provide a level of protection if you are hesitant to speak up publicly.

Another significant aspect of creating a supportive emotional environment is encouraging diversity of thought. Cultivating a space that welcomes differing opinions sparks creativity and innovation, leading to better problem-solving solutions. When individuals feel comfortable sharing their unique perspectives, it enriches the group's collective wisdom. Encouraging diversity of thought involves actively seeking out and valuing different viewpoints. For example, during brainstorming sessions, leaders can invite input from all members and appreciate diverse contributions. This practice enhances creativity and promotes inclusivity, which ensures that each person feels respected and heard.

Balancing Personal Needs and Shared Responsibilities

Finding harmony between personal aspirations and collective obligations is crucial for promoting a supportive emotional environment. This balance ensures you can pursue your goals while contributing meaningfully to your group's success. Achieving this harmony involves several strategies focusing on assessment techniques, collaborative planning, effective time management practices, and embracing flexibility.

Assessment Techniques

To begin with, regular self-reflection and group assessments play a pivotal role in understanding individual capabilities and group dynamics. Self-reflection allows you to evaluate your strengths and weaknesses and progress toward personal goals. As discussed in earlier chapters, simple techniques such as journaling or mindfulness exercises are invaluable for gaining insights into one's emotions and motivations. For instance, setting aside a few minutes each day to jot down thoughts about what went well and what could improve fosters a deeper awareness of personal growth.

Group assessments, on the other hand, provide a platform for team members to collectively evaluate their performance. Tools like anonymous surveys or facilitated group discussions can help assess collective progress without singling out individuals. These assessments can reveal strengths and areas for development within the group, ensuring that everyone understands the limits and capabilities of their peers. Creating an environment where honest feedback is given and received openly allows you and your team to develop a mutual understanding that supports emotional intelligence.

Collaborative Planning

Next, collaborative planning is essential for aligning individual contributions with overarching team goals. Using collaborative tools such as project management software or shared documents streamlines communication and ensures all voices are heard. Brainstorming sessions, where team members come together to discuss ideas freely, promote a sense of inclusivity and creativity. Such sessions should encourage all members to share their perspectives, thus ensuring diverse viewpoints are considered when planning projects or initiatives.

An example of effective collaborative planning is organizing a weekly meeting where each team member can present their progress and voice any concerns or suggestions. This practice keeps everyone informed while building a sense of ownership and accountability. Incorporating visual aids like flowcharts or mind maps also helps illustrate complex plans clearly, which makes it easier for team members to see how their contributions fit into the bigger picture.

Time Management Practices

Effective time management practices are another critical component in balancing personal and collective goals. Implementing scheduling techniques helps individuals prioritize tasks and manage their workload efficiently. One widely used method is the Eisenhower Matrix, which categorizes tasks into four quadrants based on urgency and importance. This technique helps you focus on what matters while delegating or deferring less critical tasks.

Additionally, time blocking can be beneficial for allocating specific periods throughout the day for focused work on key tasks. Setting clear boundaries for different activities enables you to strike a balance between personal pursuits and team commitments. For example, dedicating certain hours for uninterrupted work on individual projects and separate blocks for collaborative tasks ensures that you don't neglect either aspect.

Prioritizing tasks also becomes easier with to-do lists, which you can periodically review and adjust according to changing priorities. Including deadlines and milestones in these lists provides a clear roadmap for achieving individual and collective objectives. Furthermore, adopting digital tools like calendar apps or task managers can help track progress and stay organized. When everyone in the group practices good time management, it reduces stress and enhances overall productivity, creating a more supportive environment.

Flexibility and Adaptability

Finally, cultivating flexibility and adaptability is vital when dealing with the inevitable shift in priorities within any group dynamic. Recognizing that changes are natural allows you to embrace them rather than resist them, contributing to a more resilient atmosphere. Flexibility means being open to adjusting plans or approaches based on new information or circumstances, while adaptability involves developing the skills to handle these changes effectively.

One way to promote adaptability is by encouraging continuous learning and skill development. Workshops, training sessions, or online courses can empower team members to acquire new competencies that enhance their ability to handle diverse challenges. For instance, learning conflict resolution techniques can equip individuals to address disputes constructively, maintaining harmony within the group.

Another practical approach is establishing contingency plans outlining how the team will respond to unexpected events. These plans should be regularly revisited and updated to reflect any changes in the team's context or resources. Anticipating potential disruptions and preparing accordingly enables teams to maintain stability and function smoothly even when facing obstacles.

Creating a supportive atmosphere also involves showing empathy and understanding toward others' needs and circumstances. Leaders and team members alike should practice active listening, validating each other's experiences and offering support when needed. Simple gestures like acknowledging someone's hard work or offering assistance during busy periods can significantly boost morale and reinforce a sense of community.

Nurturing Collective Resilience

Fostering resilience in groups by leveraging collective strengths and support systems is essential for creating a supportive emotional environment. One primary method to achieve this is through resilience training, where workshops and storytelling sessions play pivotal roles. In these settings, individuals come together to share their experiences, successes, and challenges. Storytelling, in particular, helps build camaraderie by allowing group members to bond over common themes and learn from each other's resilience strategies.

For example, consider a team where members regularly participate in resilience workshops. During these sessions, they engage in activities designed to develop problem-solving skills, emotional regulation, and stress management techniques. Participants may share personal stories of overcoming adversity, providing practical insights, and inspiring others within the group. As a result, members feel more connected and better equipped to face future challenges together. This collective learning process nurtures an environment where everyone feels valued and supported, fostering individual and group growth.

Developing well-structured crisis response plans is another crucial aspect of building resilience within groups. Clearly defining roles and establishing effective communication channels enables groups to respond more efficiently during crises. Scenario planning, which involves simulating potential crises and practicing responses, can significantly improve a group's preparedness.

Celebrating milestones is another powerful tactic for reinforcing a supportive emotional environment. You can do this by acknowledging progress, whether it's reaching a project milestone or personal achievements. Take, for instance, a workplace that celebrates employee accomplishments monthly. These could range from completing a major project to personal milestones like reaching a fitness goal. The company might host a small gathering where achievements are publicly recognized, and team members join the celebration. Such practices boost morale and also reinforce the notion that every contribution matters. Regularly acknowledging and celebrating success creates room for the group to cultivate a positive atmosphere where individuals feel motivated and appreciated, promoting ongoing collaboration and resilience.

In this chapter, we have explored the various methods to cultivate a supportive environment that promotes personal and mutual growth. Establishing strong connections within your community and leveraging external networks helps you build relationships that encourage emotional resilience. When you nurture them with regular check-ins and shared experiences, these connections provide a solid support system. We also highlighted the importance of being mindful and intentional in your networking efforts, as this ensures genuine and meaningful bonds rather than superficial talk. Embracing these principles gives you a better chance at creating networks that promote personal growth.

Chapter 10: Continuous Improvement and Future Steps

Continuous improvement in emotional intelligence is a lifelong journey that requires dedication and self-reflection. Striving to enhance your emotional skills enables you to better deal with the complexities of relationships and manage the stresses of daily life. This chapter provides insights into how maintaining a growth mindset can propel you toward continuous development.

In this chapter, you will explore various techniques to sustain progress in developing emotional intelligence. These include leveraging tools such as self-assessment reports and journaling to maintain high levels of self-awareness. You will also learn the importance of gaining perspectives from trusted colleagues and mentors and the value of setting specific, achievable goals. Practical examples illustrate how these methods can be applied in real-life scenarios to foster ongoing improvement in emotional intelligence, ensuring that you continue to evolve and refine your skills.

Recognizing Areas for Continuous Improvement

Identifying personal areas where you can further enhance emotional intelligence is pivotal to promoting lifelong growth.

This approach contributes to continuous improvement and empowers you to manage relationships and stress more effectively. To achieve this, you can employ various strategies that encourage the overall development of emotional intelligence.

Regular self-assessments are vital in cultivating ongoing self-awareness necessary for improvement. These assessments reflect your current emotional states, responses, and patterns. For instance, tools like emotional intelligence self-assessment reports offer valuable insights into your strengths and areas needing attention (Tariq et al., 2024). Periodically retaking these assessments allows you to track your progress and identify new areas for development, and that helps maintain a high level of self-awareness, which is the foundation for sound emotional intelligence.

Gaining perspectives from others highlights blind spots that may not be evident to you. You may often overlook certain behaviors or reactions that others might easily notice. Soliciting feedback from trusted colleagues, mentors, or friends provides an external perspective that can uncover these blind spots.

Writing helps to crystallize thoughts and emotions, revealing patterns that need attention. Journaling, for example, encourages introspection and reflection. Writing down your daily experiences, feelings, and reactions helps you observe recurring themes and behaviors that may need adjustment. Journaling serves as a tool for deeper understanding and emotional clarity. It allows you to articulate your inner thoughts and emotions, which makes it easier to identify areas where you can improve emotional intelligence. This practice of regular writing leads to meaningful insights and actionable steps toward personal development.

Self-reflective practices play a significant role in identifying areas for growth. Taking time for introspection allows you to delve deeper into your thoughts and feelings. Reflecting on past experiences, achievements, and challenges can provide valuable insights into areas requiring further development. For example, after a stressful encounter at work, taking a moment to reflect on your emotional response and its impact on others can help identify patterns that need change. This level of self-awareness is instrumental in continuous emotional growth and improvement.

Soliciting feedback should be an ongoing effort rather than a one-time activity. Regularly asking for input from different sources ensures a well-rounded understanding of one's emotional intelligence. To get a comprehensive view, feedback should be sought from people in various contexts, such as work, home, and social settings. This diverse feedback can reveal different dimensions of emotional intelligence that might go unnoticed if only considered from a single perspective. Each piece of feedback contributes to a fuller picture, highlighting strengths and areas needing improvement.

Setting milestones is essential for maintaining momentum in personal development. Regular self-assessments, gaining perspectives from others, writing for reflection, and setting specific goals form the cornerstones of continuous improvement in emotional intelligence. Embracing these practices encourages a mindset of lifelong growth and allows you to refine your emotional skills continually. Committing to these strategies equips you to better manage stress, enhance your relationships, and improve interpersonal communications.

Embracing a cycle of self-assessment and feedback is essential for sustained emotional growth. This cycle begins with an internal evaluation followed by incorporating external feedback. Developing self-awareness through journaling and reflective writing supports this process by providing tangible evidence of progress and areas needing attention. Setting SMART goals ensures clarity and focus, while breaking these goals into manageable milestones keeps the process achievable and motivating.

Establishing Long-Term EQ Goals

Creating sustainable goals for enhancing EQ is crucial for ongoing personal development. To embark on this journey, it's essential to understand that setting specific and measurable goals can significantly clarify objectives and enhance focus. When our goals are vividly defined and broken down into measurable components, we gain a clearer perspective on what steps must be taken. This specificity helps transform abstract aspirations into tangible actions, making the path to improvement more manageable and less overwhelming.

For example, instead of vaguely aiming to "improve communication skills," a more effective goal might be to "practice active listening techniques in daily conversations for at least 15 minutes each day." This shift from general to specific makes the objective clear and provides a concrete activity to focus on. As a result, monitoring progress and staying motivated becomes easier, knowing exactly what needs to be achieved and how to go about it.

Visual representations of goals can also play a significant role in reinforcing commitment and aspiration. Vision boards, for instance, are powerful tools that allow you to bring your goals to life visually. A collage of images, words, and affirmations that represent your goals creates a constant visual reminder of what you are working toward. This daily visual cue helps keep your goals at the forefront of your mind, serving as a source of inspiration and motivation. When you see your aspirations on display, it reinforces your commitment to achieving them, making it harder to lose sight of your objectives.

Progress reflection is another critical aspect of sustaining emotional development. Regularly reviewing your journey allows you to assess what has been working well and what might need adjustment. It provides an opportunity to celebrate small victories, which fuels motivation and boosts confidence. Moreover, reflection encourages a growth mindset, where you acknowledge setbacks as learning experiences. Periodically evaluating your progress enables you to make informed adjustments to your goals and ensure they remain relevant and attainable. This continuous cycle of setting, reflecting, and adjusting creates a dynamic process of growth and improvement.

Incorporating an accountability partner into this process can further enhance commitment and provide the necessary motivation to stay on track. An accountability partner is someone who shares similar goals and is committed to mutual support throughout the journey. This relationship fosters a sense of responsibility, as having someone to report progress to adds a layer of external motivation. The encouragement and feedback from an accountability partner can be invaluable, especially during challenging times. They can provide different perspectives, suggest new strategies, and help maintain focus when distractions arise.

To illustrate, consider two friends, Sarah and Mark, both aiming to boost their emotional intelligence. They decide to become accountability partners, meeting weekly to discuss their progress, share challenges, and celebrate achievements. This regular interaction keeps them both engaged and focused on their goals. Knowing they have to update each other on their progress encourages them to stay diligent in their efforts, turning the pursuit of emotional intelligence into a shared journey rather than a solitary endeavor.

When setting EQ goals, adopting the SMART goal framework is also beneficial. For instance, rather than setting a broad goal like "becoming better at managing stress," a more effective SMART goal might be, "Practice deep breathing exercises for 10 minutes every morning for the next three months." This goal is specific (deep breathing exercises), measurable (10 minutes every morning), achievable (a realistic time frame and activity), relevant (directly related to stress management), and time-bound (for the next three months). Adhering to these criteria enables you to create structured goals that increase the likelihood of sustained commitment and success.

Regular progress reviews are equally important in this context. Establishing a routine for self-assessment, such as monthly reflections or quarterly evaluations, can provide valuable insights into one's development. During these reviews, it's helpful to ask reflective questions like, "What progress have I made toward my goals?", "What obstacles have I encountered, and how have I addressed them?" and "What changes can I make to improve my approach?". These questions facilitate deeper understanding and continuous refinement of strategies, ensuring that the pursuit of emotional intelligence remains dynamic and responsive to personal growth.

Another effective strategy is creating vision boards. Using vision boards to visualize goals significantly reinforces commitment and inspires continued effort. Gathering images and words that resonate with desired outcomes enables you to create a tangible representation of your aspirations. This visual tool serves as a daily reminder of what you are striving for, and that helps maintain motivation.

Accountability partnerships also play a pivotal role in maintaining motivation and commitment. Having a trusted friend or mentor to share goals with can provide an added layer of support and accountability. This partnership can involve regular check-ins, where both parties discuss their progress, celebrate successes, and brainstorm solutions for any challenges. An accountability partner can offer encouragement, provide constructive feedback, and remind each other of their long-term aspirations. This reciprocal relationship enhances the likelihood of staying on track and persevering through difficulties.

Journaling is another practical tool for tracking progress and fostering self-reflection. Keeping a goal-setting journal allows you to document your goals, action plans, and milestones. Reflecting on the journey through journaling helps identify patterns, recognize areas of improvement, and celebrate achievements. Moreover, writing down thoughts and emotions can provide clarity and insight, aiding in better understanding your progress.

Leveraging New Technologies for Growth

Technology has become an essential tool in enhancing emotional intelligence skills and supporting ongoing development. Leveraging various technological tools enables you to improve your self-awareness, gain practical skills in emotional intelligence, and find supportive communities to share experiences.

Apps for self-reflection are particularly valuable in encouraging regular emotional check-ins, which promote self-awareness. For instance, digital journals or mood-tracking apps let users record their feelings and thoughts throughout the day. By doing so, you can identify patterns in your emotions and behaviors, which helps you understand triggers and responses. Such consistent self-monitoring promotes greater self-awareness while encouraging proactive emotional regulation.

Online courses and webinars offer another avenue for enhancing emotional intelligence. These platforms provide access to diverse content that deepens understanding and practical application of emotional intelligence principles. Interactive online classes on topics like empathy, communication, and conflict resolution allow learners to engage with material at their own pace. Webinars conducted by psychology and personal development experts offer insights grounded in research and practice, which viewers can apply in real-life scenarios. Access to such varied educational resources builds a robust foundation in emotional intelligence, equipping you with skills essential for personal and professional success.

Digital support groups and forums create spaces where you can share your experiences in an empathetic environment. Platforms like social media groups or specialized forums for emotional intelligence enthusiasts encourage community interaction and provide mutual support. Engaging with others who are also working on improving their emotional intelligence can be highly motivating. Participants can discuss their progress, exchange tips, and offer encouragement, creating a sense of camaraderie and shared purpose. This collective experience reinforces learning and helps members feel supported, enhancing their social awareness and empathy.

Podcasts have become a convenient way to integrate emotional intelligence learning into daily routines. Many podcasts cover a wide range of topics related to emotional intelligence, from stress management and mindfulness to relationship skills and self-regulation. These podcasts often feature interviews with experts, discussions on practical strategies, and guided exercises that listeners can apply in their lives. Because you can listen to them while commuting, exercising, or doing household chores, podcasts make it easy to continually learn and grow your emotional intelligence, even with a busy schedule.

Moreover, technology enables accessing diverse content, which significantly enhances the understanding and practical skills of emotional intelligence. Various multimedia formats, such as videos, articles, and interactive modules, cater to different learning preferences, making emotional intelligence concepts accessible to a broader audience. Video content, for instance, can demonstrate real-life scenarios and effective communication techniques, providing visual learners with relatable examples. Articles and blogs written by thought leaders in emotional intelligence offer in-depth analyses and personal anecdotes that enrich the reader's knowledge and application of EI principles. Interactive modules and simulations allow users to practice their skills in a controlled environment, giving them the confidence to apply these techniques in real life.

Regular use of these tools fosters continuous improvement and deepens your competence in emotional intelligence. Apps for self-reflection serve as daily reminders to check in with yourself, promoting a habit of mindfulness and emotional literacy. Online courses and webinars expand your theoretical and practical understanding, providing a structured yet flexible learning path. Digital support groups create a network of like-minded individuals who offer encouragement and share valuable insights, enhancing relational skills. Podcasts seamlessly integrate learning into daily life, ensuring that emotional intelligence development is an ongoing process rather than a one-off effort.

Furthermore, technology facilitates personalized learning experiences. Algorithms in many educational apps and platforms can tailor content to individual needs and progress levels. For instance, an app might suggest specific articles, videos, or exercises based on a user's previous activities and assessments. This customization ensures learners focus on areas where they need the most improvement, making their efforts more effective.

In workplaces, emotionally intelligent leadership can be bolstered through technology. Companies can implement training programs using online platforms offering interactive and engaging emotional intelligence modules. These programs can be integrated into the company's learning management systems, ensuring employees at all levels can access valuable EQ training. As organizations continue to recognize the importance of emotional intelligence in leadership, incorporating it into employee development programs becomes increasingly critical (Maldonado & Márquez, 2023).

Moreover, technology offers scalable solutions for emotional intelligence training. Where logistics and costs might limit traditional training methods, digital tools can reach a global audience efficiently. This scalability is particularly beneficial for multinational companies looking to standardize EI training across different locations. With the help of technology, such organizations can deliver consistent training quality, track progress, and measure outcomes effectively.

Joining Communities for Mutual Support

Building meaningful connections with others plays a crucial role in the ongoing development of emotional intelligence. Interacting with diverse individuals enables you to continually expand your empathy, enhancing your ability to handle various social landscapes. Here, we explore several avenues that facilitate such connections and contribute to emotional growth.

Networking opportunities through gatherings create a platform for meeting like-minded individuals with similar goals and aspirations. Whether attending local EQ workshops or seminars, these settings offer fertile ground for forging new relationships. Engaging in face-to-face conversations can deepen our understanding of different perspectives and foster a sense of community. These interactions help share knowledge and provide emotional support, which is vital for personal growth.

Online communities have become an essential resource for continuous improvement in emotional intelligence. Social media groups and forums dedicated to emotional intelligence discussions offer a virtual space where people can exchange ideas and experiences. These platforms provide access to a myriad of resources, including articles, webinars, and podcasts that enrich our understanding of emotional intelligence. Being part of such online communities ensures that you are never alone on your journey, as there is always someone available to offer advice or share their insights.

Mentorship is another powerful tool for emotional growth. Connecting with a mentor allows you to benefit from the experience and wisdom of someone further along in their journey. Peer mentorship programs enable you to receive personalized guidance tailored to your specific needs and challenges. A mentor can provide valuable feedback, helping you recognize areas for improvement and encouraging accountability. Through this relationship, you not only gain practical advice but also develop a deeper sense of empathy and understanding by observing how your mentor navigates their emotional landscape.

Volunteering offers an unparalleled opportunity to cultivate empathy and social awareness. Engaging with community projects, especially those involving youth or marginalized groups, exposes you to diverse situations requiring adaptability and resilience. Volunteer opportunities allow you to step into others' shoes, experiencing their struggles and triumphs firsthand. This direct engagement fosters a deeper connection with the community and enhances your ability to empathize with others. Moreover, volunteering often involves teamwork, allowing you to build strong interpersonal relationships and improve your communication skills.

To illustrate, consider participating in a local youth mentoring program. Volunteering with organizations like Big Brothers of Greater Vancouver can expose you to various challenging situations that require creative problem-solving. For instance, mentors may need to bridge communication gaps or address the unique needs of each mentee. Overcoming these challenges hones your problem-solving abilities and builds confidence, preparing you to tackle obstacles in professional environments. Additionally, the networking and community engagement aspects of volunteering enhance your reputation as a community-oriented individual, an attractive quality to many employers.

Reflecting on personal experiences within these environments can lead to significant emotional growth. For instance, actively participating in volunteer events and meetings maximizes your networking opportunities, fostering meaningful professional connections. These connections open doors to potential career opportunities, provide emotional nourishment, and reinforce your commitment to social responsibility.

In summary, building connections through various means, such as networking events, online communities, mentorship, and volunteering, facilitates the continuous improvement of emotional intelligence. Each avenue provides unique benefits, from gaining new perspectives and resources to developing empathy and social awareness. Actively participating in these activities and reflecting on your experiences helps ensure ongoing emotional growth and refinement of your skills.

Reflecting on the insights shared in this chapter, it's clear that the journey toward improving emotional intelligence is ongoing and deeply personal. Embracing self-assessment tools and seeking feedback from others can help uncover blind spots and encourage deeper understanding. Journaling and setting specific, actionable goals provide a structured approach to continuous improvement. These practices promote a growth mindset, allowing individuals to evolve their emotional skills continually and effectively.

Committing to regular reflection and setting realistic milestones helps ensure that your emotional development remains dynamic and responsive to personal growth. Engaging with others through mentorship or community support further solidifies these efforts through encouragement and diverse perspectives. Ultimately, the path to greater emotional intelligence improves personal well-being, relationships, and resilience.

Conclusion

As we draw this journey to a close, let's take a moment to reflect on what we've covered and its implications for personal development and professional advancement. We've discussed what emotional intelligence entails and explored its components, such as self-awareness, self-regulation, motivation, empathy, and social skills, all of which shape how we interact with ourselves and others.

Throughout this book, we've uncovered how improving emotional intelligence can drastically improve your daily interactions, facilitate better decision-making, and promote a more peaceful work environment. Recognizing and managing your emotions equips you to approach challenges with a balanced perspective and to handle conflicts better.

The importance of continuous growth cannot be overstated. Developing emotional intelligence is not a one-time achievement but an ongoing process that requires consistent effort and mindfulness. Just like learning any new skill, it involves practice, patience, and perseverance. Embrace the journey of self-improvement with enthusiasm, knowing that each experience, whether positive or negative, is an opportunity to refine your emotional intelligence further.

Remember that practical application is essential. The insights and strategies you've gained are powerful tools that can reshape your life, but they require action to bring about change. Integrate these practices into your daily routine and watch how these habits will reinforce your emotional intelligence over time. The changes might seem subtle at first, but you'll notice an improvement in how you perceive and react to situations.

Now, let's turn our attention inward. As you close this book, take a moment to reflect on your personal goals and think about how you envision integrating emotional intelligence into your daily life. What specific areas would you like to focus on?

Whatever your objectives, I encourage you to take immediate action. Choose one emotion that often challenges you and commit to exploring it more deeply. Observe when it arises, examine its triggers, and experiment with different strategies to manage it constructively. Alternatively, reach out to someone with whom you'd like to strengthen your relationship. Initiate a conversation grounded in empathy and openness while expressing your genuine intention to understand and connect.

Remember, the real change happens outside the pages of this book. It's in those everyday moments when you consciously choose to apply what you've learned. Your dedication to practicing emotional intelligence will yield transformative results and create a ripple effect, inspiring others to seek emotional growth.

In conclusion, I challenge you to commit wholeheartedly to this path of personal and professional development. Trust the lifelong process of nurturing your emotional intelligence and acknowledge that each step forward brings you closer to becoming the best version of yourself. The potential for positive change is boundless, and it starts with a single, intentional action. Take that step today, and watch as you unlock new levels of connection and success!

References

A quote by Anthony Robbins. (n.d.). Goodreads. https://www.goodreads.com/quotes/363827-the-quality-of-your-life-is-in-direct-proportion-to

A quote by Elizabeth Gilbert. (n.d.). Goodreads. https://www.goodreads.com/quotes/31763-your-emotions-are-the-slaves-to-your-thoughts-and-you

A quote by John Hancock. (n.d.). Forbes. https://www.forbes.com/quotes/5269/

A quote by Lou Holtz. (n.d.). Goodreads. https://www.goodreads.com/quotes/21657-it-s-not-the-load-that-breaks-you-down-it-s-the

A quote by Mohsin Hamid. (n.d.). Goodreads.com. https://www.goodreads.com/quotes/9076745-empathy-is-about-finding-echoes-of-another-person-in-yourself

A quote by Steve Jobs. (n.d.). Goodreads. https://www.goodreads.com/quotes/772887-the-only-way-to-do-great-work-is-to-love

Antonopoulou, H. (2024). *The value of emotional intelligence: Self-Awareness, self-regulation, motivation, and empathy as key components.* Technium Education and Humanities, 8, 78–92. https://doi.org/10.47577/teh.v8i.9719

Ask Huberman Lab. (2018). *Ask Huberman Lab.* https://ai.hubermanlab.com/s/6b_Jj3bC

Autieri, A. (2023, August 10). *Understanding the Science of Stress: How It Affects Your Mind and Body - Advanced Women's Health Clinics.* https://www.advancedwomenshealth.ca/blog/understanding-the-science-of-stress-how-it-affects-your-mind-and-body

Badri, M. A., Alkhaili, M., Aldhaheri, H., Yang, G., Albahar, M., & Alrashdi, A. (2022, March 17). Exploring the Reciprocal Relationships between Happiness and Life Satisfaction of Working Adults—Evidence from Abu Dhabi. *International Journal of Environmental Research and Public Health.* https://doi.org/10.3390/ijerph19063575

Cavaness, K., Picchioni, A., & Fleshman, J. W. (2020). Linking emotional intelligence to successful health care leadership: The big five model of personality. *Clinics in Colon and Rectal Surgery, 33*(04), 195–203. NCBI. https://doi.org/10.1055/s-0040-1709435

Cherry, K. (2023, December 13). *Extrinsic vs. Intrinsic Motivation: What's the Difference?* https://www.verywellmind.com/differences-between-extrinsic-and-intrinsic-motivation-2795384

Chowdhury, M. R. (2019, January 22). *What is Emotional Resilience and How to Build It?* https://positivepsychology.com/emotional-resilience/

Chu, B., Marwaha, K., Ayers, D., & Sanvictores, T. (2024). *Physiology, stress reaction.* PubMed; StatPearls Publishing. https://www.ncbi.nlm.nih.gov/books/NBK541120/

Developing Emotional Intelligence through Mentorship Programs. (n.d.). https://fastercapital.com/content/Developing-Emotional-Intelligence-through-Mentorship-Programs.html

Developing Social Skills in Leadership. (2024, April 2). https://www.leadernavigation.com/social-skills

Drigas, A., Papoutsi, C., & Skianis, C. (2023). Being an emotionally intelligent leader through the nine-layer model of emotional intelligence—the supporting role of new technologies. *Sustainability, 15*(10), 8103. MDPI. https://www.mdpi.com/2071-1050/15/10/8103

Emotional Intelligence Consortium. (n.d.). *Articles, Research and Information on Emotional Intelligence*. https://www.eiconsortium.org/

Emotional intelligence self-assessment. (2021, January 29). https://www.workplacestrategiesformentalhealth.com/resources/emotional-intelligence-self-assessment

Farrahi, H., Kafi, S. M., Karimi, T., & Delazar, R. (2015). Emotional intelligence and its relationship with general health among the students of University of Guilan, Iran. *Iranian Journal of Psychiatry and Behavioral Sciences, 9*(3). https://doi.org/10.17795/ijpbs-1582

FasterCapital. (n.d.). *Emotional intelligence: Peer support networks: The role of peer support networks in emotional intelligence*. https://fastercapital.com/content/Emotional-Intelligence--Peer-Support-Networks---The-Role-of-Peer-Support-Networks-in-

FasterCapital. (n.d.). *Self-awareness practices: Goal setting: Setting goals with intention: A self-aware approach.* https://fastercapital.com/content/Self-awareness-Practices--Goal-Setting--Setting-Goals-with-Intention--A-Self-aware-Approach.html

Top 6 Emotional Intelligence Podcasts. (2024). https://goodpods.com/leaderboard/top-100-shows-by-category/other/emotional-intelligence

Hostinar, C. E., & Gunnar, M. R. (2015). Social support can buffer against stress and shape brain activity. *AJOB Neuroscience, 6*(3), 34–42. https://doi.org/10.1080/21507740.2015.1047054

Houston, E. (2019, February 6). *The Importance of Emotional Intelligence (Including EI Quotes).* https://positivepsychology.com/importance-of-emotional-intelligence/

How Emotional Intelligence Helps Your Professional Growth. (2024, July 26). https://managementconcepts.com/resource/how-emotional-intelligence-helps-your-professional-growth/

How Local Volunteering Can Shape Your Career Path. (2024, February 27). https://www.bigbrothersvancouver.com/inspiring-stories/how-volunteering-can-shape-your-career/

How To Develop Conflict Resolution Skills: 7 Easy Steps. (2024, July 17).

https://www.personatalent.com/development/how-to-develop-conflict-resolution-skills/

Jiménez-Picón, N., Romero-Martín, M., Ponce-Blandón, J. A., Ramirez-Baena, L., Palomo-Lara, J. C., & Gómez-Salgado, J. (2021, May 20). The Relationship between Mindfulness and Emotional Intelligence as a Protective Factor for Healthcare Professionals: Systematic Review. *International Journal of Environmental Research and Public Health.* https://doi.org/10.3390/ijerph18105491

Khatibi, A., I Jackson, P., Rainville, P., & Jauniaux, J. (2019). *A meta-analysis of neuroimaging studies on pain empathy: Investigating the role of visual information and observers' perspective.* Social Cognitive and Affective Neuroscience. https://doi.org/10.1093/scan/nsz055

Kriakous, S. A., Elliott, K. A., Lamers, C., & Owen, R. (2020). The effectiveness of mindfulness-based stress reduction on the psychological functioning of healthcare professionals: A systematic review. *Mindfulness, 12*(1). https://doi.org/10.1007/s12671-020-01500-9

Lee, C.-C., Yeh, W.-C., Yu, Z., & Lin, X.-C. (2023). The relationships between leader emotional intelligence, transformational leadership, and transactional leadership and job performance: A mediator model of trust. *Heliyon, 9*(8). https://doi.org/10.1016/j.heliyon.2023.e18007

Luna, L. M. B. -, Vilar, M. M. -, Soto, C. M. -, & Santiago, J. L. C. -. (2021). Emotional Intelligence Measures: A Systematic Review. *Healthcare, 9*(12), 1696. https://doi.org/10.3390/healthcare9121696

Maldonado, I. C., & Márquez, M.-D. B. (2023). Emotional intelligence, leadership, and work teams: A hybrid literature review. *Heliyon, 9*(10). https://doi.org/10.1016/j.heliyon.2023.e20356

Mayo Clinic. (2022, August 3). *Exercise and stress: Get Moving to Manage Stress.* https://www.mayoclinic.org/healthy-lifestyle/stress-management/in-depth/exercise-and-stress/art-20044469

McEwen, B. S. (2017, April 10). Neurobiological and systemic effects of chronic stress. *Chronic Stress.* https://doi.org/10.1177/2470547017692328

McManus, M. R. (2023, March 31). *Chronic stress can affect your health.* https://www.cnn.com/2023/03/31/health/exercises-to-reduce-stress-wellness/index.html

Miao, C., Humphrey, R. H., & Qian, S. (2016). A meta-analysis of emotional intelligence and work attitudes. *Journal of Occupational and Organizational Psychology, 90*(2), 177–202. https://doi.org/10.1111/joop.12167

Moeller, R. W., Seehuus, M., & Peisch, V. (2020). Emotional intelligence, belongingness, and mental health in college students. *Frontiers in Psychology, 11*(93). https://doi.org/10.3389/fpsyg.2020.00093

Morrison, T. (2006, March 30). Emotional Intelligence, Emotion and Social Work: Context, Characteristics, Complications and Contribution. *British Journal of Social Work*. https://doi.org/10.1093/bjsw/bcl016

Mowbray, P. K., Gu, J., Chen, Z., Herman, & Wilkinson, A. (2024). How do tangible and intangible rewards encourage employee voice? The perspective of dual proactive motivational pathways. *International Journal of Human Resource Management*, 1–33. https://doi.org/10.1080/09585192.2024.2353660

Ogbeiwi, O. (2017). Why written objectives need to be really SMART. *British Journal of Healthcare Management, 23*(7), 324–336. https://doi.org/10.12968/bjhc.2017.23.7.324

Parsons, D., Gardner, P., Parry, S., & Smart, S. (2021). Mindfulness-Based approaches for managing stress, anxiety and depression for health students in tertiary education: A scoping review. *Mindfulness, 13*(1). https://doi.org/10.1007/s12671-021-01740-3

Patil, D. (2024, June 12). *The role of emotional intelligence in achieving success: A key to personal and professional growth*. Medium. https://patildilip23.medium.com/the-role-of-emotional-intelligence-in-achieving-success-a-key-to-personal-and-professional-growth-c58f673e53a8

Popular Blog BD. (2024, July 10). *Goal Setting for Success: Creating a Roadmap for Your Future.* https://www.salewad.com/goal-setting-for-success-creating-a-roadmap-for-your-future/

Rey. (2024, April 5). 18 *Tips On How to Stay Disciplined During Tough Times.* https://misterindependent.com/how-to-stay-disciplined-during-tough-times/

Rheanna. (n.d.). *The importance of emotional intelligence in the workplace.* University Canada West (UCW).

https://www.ucanwest.ca/blog/education-careers-tips/the-importance-of-emotional-intelligence-in-the-workplace/

Riversoftware. (2024, March 22). *Defining Success: A Comprehensive Guide to Goal Setting. River.* https://www.riversoftware.com/uncategorized/defining-success-a-comprehensive-guide-to-goal-setting/

Rogue, A. (2021, September 14). *Understanding the Difference Between Intrinsic and Extrinsic Motivations.* Talentoday. https://www.talentoday.com/blog/understanding-the-difference-between-intrinsic-and-extrinsic-motivations/

Schuman-Olivier, Z., Trombka, M., Lovas, D. A., Brewer, J. A., Vago, D. R., Gawande, R., Dunne, J. P., Lazar, S. W., Loucks, E. B., & Fulwiler, C. (2020). *Mindfulness and behavior change.* Harvard Review of Psychiatry. https://doi.org/10.1097/HRP.0000000000000277

Segal, J., Smith, M., Robinson, L., & Shubin, J. (2024, February 5). *Improving Emotional Intelligence.* https://www.helpguide.org/articles/mental-health/emotional-intelligence-eq.htm

Setting Goals: The Blueprint for Personal and Professional Achievement. (n.d.). https://www.graygroupintl.com/blog/setting-goals

Sevinc, G., Rusche, J., Wong, B., Datta, T., Kaufman, R., Gutz, S. E., Schneider, M., Todorova, N., Gaser, C., Thomalla, G., Rentz, D., Dickerson, B. D., & Lazar, S. W. (2021). Mindfulness training improves cognition and strengthens intrinsic connectivity between the hippocampus and posteromedial cortex in healthy older adults. *Frontiers in Aging Neuroscience, 13*. https://doi.org/10.3389/fnagi.2021.702796

Stefanic, D. (2024, March 27). *Emotional Intelligence in the workplace.* https://hyperspace.mv/emotional-intelligence-in-the-workplace/

Stoewen, D. L. (2024). The vital connection between emotional intelligence and well-being - Part 1: Understanding emotional intelligence and why it matters. *The Canadian Veterinary Journal = La Revue Veterinaire Canadienne, 65*(2), 182–184. https://www.ncbi.nlm.nih.gov/pmc/articles/PMC10783582/

Suman, C. (2023). *Cultivating a growth-oriented mindset in educational settings.* Zenodo (CERN European Organization for Nuclear Research). https://doi.org/10.5281/zenodo.8154509

Suny Geneseo. (2018, August 3). *Memorable Quotations I Have Found.* https://www.geneseo.edu/sites/default/files/users/user114/VPBonfiglio_Quotes.pdf

Tariq, Ahmad, Bhat, Chahal, & Dinesh. (2024). *The power of emotional intelligence: An overview and analysis of key concepts.*

The Importance of Emotional Intelligence in Professional Growth. (n.d.). ChenMed. https://careers.chenmed.com/us/en/blogarticle/the-importance-of-emotional-intelligence-in-professional-growth

The Power of Emotional Intelligence in Relationships. (2023, August 3). https://care-clinics.com/the-power-of-emotional-intelligence-in-relationships/

Turakitwanakan, W., Mekseepralard, C., & Busarakumtragul, P. (2013). Effects of mindfulness meditation on serum cortisol of medical students. *Journal of the Medical Association of Thailand = Chotmaihet Thangphaet, 96 Suppl 1*, S90-95. https://pubmed.ncbi.nlm.nih.gov/23724462/

Walinga, J. (2014, October 17). *Stress and Coping – Introduction to Psychology – 1st Canadian Edition*. https://opentextbc.ca/introductiontopsychology/chapter/15-2-stress-and-coping/

Walker, S. A., Pinkus, R. T., Olderbak, S., & MacCann, C. (2023). People with higher relationship satisfaction use more humor, valuing, and receptive listening to regulate their partners' emotions. *Current Psychology, 43*. https://doi.org/10.1007/s12144-023-04432-4

Wedgwood, J. (2019, August 29). *The Importance of Work-Life Balance*. https://thehappinessindex.com/blog/importance-work-life-balance

Weger, M., & Sandi, C. (2018). High anxiety trait: A vulnerable phenotype for stress-induced depression. *Neuroscience & Biobehavioral Reviews, 87*, 27–37. https://doi.org/10.1016/j.neubiorev.2018.01.012

Worthen, M., & Cash, E. (2023). *Stress Management.* StatPearls Publishing. https://www.ncbi.nlm.nih.gov/books/NBK513300/

Wright, K. W. (2023, June 14). *15 Ways to Cultivate Emotional Resilience.* Day One | Your Journal for Life. https://dayoneapp.com/blog/emotional-resilience/

Yamani, N., Shahabi, M., & Haghani, F. (2014). The relationship between emotional intelligence and job stress in the faculty of medicine in Isfahan university of medical sciences. *Journal of Advances in Medical Education & Professionalism,* *2*(1), 20–26. https://www.ncbi.nlm.nih.gov/pmc/articles/PMC4235538/

Moeller, R. W., Seehuus, M., & Peisch, V. (2020). Emotional intelligence, belongingness, and mental health in college students. *Frontiers in Psychology,* *11*(93). https://doi.org/10.3389/fpsyg.2020.00093

Morrison, T. (2006, March 30). *Emotional Intelligence, Emotion and Social Work: Context, Characteristics, Complications and Contribution.* British Journal of Social Work. https://doi.org/10.1093/bjsw/bcl016

Parsons, D., Gardner, P., Parry, S., & Smart, S. (2021, September 11). *Mindfulness-Based Approaches for Managing Stress, Anxiety and Depression for Health Students in Tertiary Education: a Scoping Review.* Mindfulness. https://doi.org/10.1007/s12671-021-01740-3

Popular Blog BD. (2024, July 10). *Goal Setting for Success: Creating a Roadmap for Your Future - Popular Blog BD.* Popular Blog

BD. https://www.salewad.com/goal-setting-for-success-creating-a-roadmap-for-your-future/

Popular Blog BD. (2024, July 10). *Goal Setting for Success: Creating a Roadmap for Your Future - Popular Blog BD*. Popular Blog BD. https://www.salewad.com/goal-setting-for-success-creating-a-roadmap-for-your-future/

ROGUE, A. (2021, September 14). Understanding the Difference Between Intrinsic and Extrinsic Motivations. Talentoday. https://www.talentoday.com/blog/understanding-the-difference-between-intrinsic-and-extrinsic-motivations/

Cherry, K. (2023, December 13). Extrinsic vs. Intrinsic Motivation: What's the Difference? Verywell Mind. https://www.verywellmind.com/differences-between-extrinsic-and-intrinsic-motivation-2795384

Personio. (n.d.). Intrinsic and Extrinsic Motivation: Difference & Best Practices. Www.personio.com. https://www.personio.com/hr-lexicon/intrinsic-and-extrinsic-motivation/

Developing Social Skills in Leadership. (2024, April 2). Leader Navigation. https://www.leadernavigation.com/social-skills

How To Develop Conflict Resolution Skills: 7 Easy Steps. (2024, July 17). https://www.personatalent.com/development/how-to-develop-conflict-resolution-skills/

Stefanic, D. (2024, March 27). Emotional Intelligence in the Workplace. https://hyperspace.mv/emotional-intelligence-in-the-workplace/

Rey. (2024, April 5). *18 Tips On How to Stay Disciplined During Tough Times.* Mister Independent; Mister Independent. https://misterindependent.com/how-to-stay-disciplined-during-tough-times/

Rheanna. (n.d.). *The importance of emotional intelligence in the workplace.* University Canada West (UCW). https://www.ucanwest.ca/blog/education-careers-tips/the-importance-of-emotional-intelligence-in-the-workplace/

Riversoftware. (2024, March 22). *Defining Success: A Comprehensive Guide to Goal Setting.* River. https://www.riversoftware.com/uncategorized/defining-success-a-comprehensive-guide-to-goal-setting/

Schuman-Olivier, Z., Trombka, M., Lovas, D. A., Brewer, J. A., Vago, D. R., Gawande, R., Dunne, J. P., Lazar, S. W., Loucks, E. B., & Fulwiler, C. (2020). *Mindfulness and behavior change.* Harvard Review of Psychiatry. https://doi.org/10.1097/HRP.0000000000000277

Segal, J., Smith, M., Robinson, L., & Shubin, J. (2024, February 5). *Improving Emotional Intelligence (EQ).* HelpGuide. https://www.helpguide.org/articles/mental-health/emotional-intelligence-eq.htm

Setting Goals: The Blueprint for Personal and Professional Achievement. (n.d.). Www.graygroupintl.com. https://www.graygroupintl.com/blog/setting-goals

Setting Goals: The Blueprint for Personal and Professional Achievement. (n.d.). Www.graygroupintl.com. https://www.graygroupintl.com/blog/setting-goals

Stoewen, D. L. (2024). The vital connection between emotional intelligence and well-being - Part 1: Understanding emotional intelligence and why it matters. *The Canadian Veterinary Journal = La Revue Veterinaire Canadienne*, *65*(2), 182–184. https://www.ncbi.nlm.nih.gov/pmc/articles/PMC10783582/#:~:text=Higher%20EQ%20means%20improved%20stress

The Importance of Emotional Intelligence in Professional Growth. (n.d.). ChenMed. https://careers.chenmed.com/us/en/blogarticle/the-importance-of-emotional-intelligence-in-professional-growth

The Power of Emotional Intelligence in Relationships. (2023, August 3). https://care-clinics.com/the-power-of-emotional-intelligence-in-relationships/

Walinga, J. (2014, October 17). *Stress and Coping – Introduction to Psychology – 1st Canadian Edition.* Opentextbc.ca. https://opentextbc.ca/introductiontopsychology/chapter/15-2-stress-and-coping/

Wedgwood, J. (2019, August 29). *The Importance of Work-Life Balance | The Happiness Index.* Thehappinessindex.com.

https://thehappinessindex.com/blog/importance-work-life-balance

Worthen, M., & Cash, E. (2023). *Stress Management.* Nih.gov; StatPearls Publishing. https://www.ncbi.nlm.nih.gov/books/NBK513300/

Wright, K. W. (2023, June 14). *15 Ways to Cultivate Emotional Resilience.* Day One | Your Journal for Life. https://dayoneapp.com/blog/emotional-resilience/

WSMH. (n.d.). WSMH. https://www.workplacestrategiesformentalhealth.com/resources/emotional-intelligence-self-assessment

WSMH. (n.d.). WSMH. https://www.workplacestrategiesformentalhealth.com/resources/emotional-intelligence-self-assessment

Made in United States
North Haven, CT
17 November 2024

60473824R00100